THE BANKS WE DESERVE

About Island Press

Since 1984, the nonprofit organization Island Press has been stimulating, shaping, and communicating ideas that are essential for solving environmental problems worldwide. With more than 1,000 titles in print and some 30 new releases each year, we are the nation's leading publisher on environmental issues. We identify innovative thinkers and emerging trends in the environmental field. We work with world-renowned experts and authors to develop cross-disciplinary solutions to environmental challenges.

Island Press designs and executes educational campaigns, in conjunction with our authors, to communicate their critical messages in print, in person, and online using the latest technologies, innovative programs, and the media. Our goal is to reach targeted audiences—scientists, policy makers, environmental advocates, urban planners, the media, and concerned citizens—with information that can be used to create the framework for long-term ecological health and human well-being.

Island Press gratefully acknowledges major support from The Bobolink Foundation, Caldera Foundation, The Curtis and Edith Munson Foundation, The Forrest C. and Frances H. Lattner Foundation, The JPB Foundation, The Kresge Foundation, The Summit Charitable Foundation, Inc., and many other generous organizations and individuals.

The opinions expressed in this book are those of the author(s) and do not necessarily reflect the views of our supporters.

The Banks We Deserve

Reclaiming Community Banking for a Just Economy

Oscar Perry Abello

ISLANDPRESS | Washington | Covelo

Library of Congress Control Number: 2024941425

All Island Press books are printed on environmentally responsible materials.

Manufactured in the United States of America
10 9 8 7 6 5 4 3 2 1

Keywords: B Corp, clean energy, climate change, community bank,
Community Development Financial Institution (CDFI), credit union,
Federal Deposit Insurance Corporation (FDIC), local bank, minority-owned
bank, racial wealth gap, redlining, renewable energy, social impact investing

To Karalyn, my partner in crime

Contents

Introduction

Every Wednesday, commercial loan officer Barbara Arroyo meets with her bank's credit committee to tell them about the lives, hopes, and dreams of her clients: small business owners in the Bronx, running everything from bodegas to barbershops to catering companies. Barbara works at Ponce Bank—one of just two community banks headquartered in the Bronx, the borough of New York City where she was born and raised, a place with 1.4 million predominantly Hispanic and Black residents.

The credit committee, which consists of the bank's chief executive officer, chief financial officer, and a few of its board members, reviews the finances and business plans for each business as well as Barbara's findings about the owner's commitment to the community and the importance of their business to the neighborhood. The credit committee knows the community too—some members have worked or served on the bank's board since the 1990s. When Barbara brings up a potential loan, a credit committee member may recall making a previous loan years ago to that same business owner or to their mother or father when they owned the business. A credit committee member may request an in-person meeting with one of Barbara's prospects. Barbara estimates that nine times out of ten the loan requests that she brings to the meeting eventually get approved, though some might take another week or even another month or two to show the credit committee members what they want to see before making a final decision.

Barbara grew up in the Edenwald public housing development in the northeast Bronx, a child of migrants from Puerto Rico who arrived in New York when they were just children themselves. Her father and mother worked two or three jobs each. During her high school years, Barbara got a summer internship at a big bank and eventually earned a full scholarship to attend college. She decided on a career in banking to help people in communities like the one where she grew up. After graduating, Barbara landed a job back at a big bank in New York City, where she found great mentors and managers—banking is still the kind of business where most of the learning happens on the job and not in a classroom—but she soon became frustrated with how things worked. Barbara was expected to produce a certain number of small business loan applications submitted from clients every month, knowing that most of them, maybe 80 percent of them, would be denied for one reason or another. Not enough collateral here, credit score too low there. She told me that she felt like "just an order-taker." It wasn't what she envisioned for herself. She wasn't given the time and space to work with clients to understand their business more deeply and get both the business and the bank to a place where an application would be approved. There wasn't any flexibility to look beyond a credit score that reflects a history of systemic racism[1] and may have little to do with the borrower's actual ability to repay a loan. Although the small business owners she was courting were mostly in and around the Bronx, Barbara could see that the clients who met the big bank's seemingly inflexible lending standards usually weren't the clients she came into banking to serve. Eventually, one of her mentors suggested that instead of trying to bring her community to a bank, maybe she needed to work for a bank that was already serving her community. She finally found what she was looking for at Ponce Bank, and she still believes it was the best professional decision she's ever made.

Barbara had heard of Ponce Bank when she was growing up, but she'd never imagined working there. From the outside, it seemed too small for her to have the kind of impact she wanted to have on her community. She thought her reach wouldn't be that far. How much could she really affect or play a part in contributing to her local community at such a comparatively smaller institution? But, as it turned out, at Ponce the impact she has on the community is, as Barbara told me, "Ten times more now. Hands down."

It's a lesson worth taking to heart for those who want to confront the big challenges this country and this planet face today, challenges that require action at every level of government, commerce, and industry, challenges like racial inequity, lack of affordable housing, and climate change. We can't wait around for giant global megabanks to swoop in and save anyone. Communities need to reclaim the power of banking.

We've never done anything big in the United States without little banks. Although community banks like Ponce have always shared the landscape with larger institutions and other kinds of investors, since the country's inception community banks have made loans to build, acquire, and maintain most of the houses, apartment buildings, storefronts, smaller office buildings, factories, and warehouses that make up the cities and communities where we live, work, play, or gather for worship and other purposes. Community banks also funded the beloved local businesses that have become pillars of so many communities from big city neighborhoods to small town main streets—and they're still a major source of small business lending today. Even when it comes to big public infrastructure projects like roads, bridges, public transit systems, water and sewer systems, and power systems, all those projects get financed using municipal bonds, many of which community banks bought on the bond market along with other investors. Community banks were once a much larger collective force in the financial system than it might seem given today's much different banking landscape, where global megabanks become more dominant every quarter.

There isn't a universally agreed-upon definition for a community bank, but generally speaking, it's a bank that focuses on a concentrated geography, like a city or a metropolitan area, or perhaps a rural county. Community banks are also characterized by their reliance on what banks call "soft information"—their knowledge of local community needs and their relationships with local businesses or local developers—to make lending decisions. Since the 1980s, community banks have fallen both in number and in market share. According to the Federal Deposit Insurance

Corporation, which regulates banks and insures bank deposits in the United States, in 1984 there were 15,767 community banks, representing 39 percent of banking industry assets.[2] By the first quarter of 2024, there were just 4,128 community banks, representing just 11.31 percent of banking industry assets.[3]

What happened to all those community banks? Financial crises took down a big chunk of them. Between 1980 and 1995, more than twenty-nine hundred mostly small community banks failed during the prolonged savings-and-loan crisis.[4] The global financial crisis that started in 2007 took down another five hundred mostly smaller banks by the end of 2014.[5] But outside of these two periods, bank failures have been quite rare since the inception of federal deposit insurance in 1934. Between 1941 and 1979, an average of 5.3 banks failed a year; between 1996 and 2006, there were an average of 4.3 bank failures per year; and between 2015 and 2022, there were an average of 3.6 bank failures a year.[6] That still leaves around eighty-three hundred community banks that were simply bought up by larger banks, which often would later get bought up by even larger banks.

The consolidation of the banking industry was a policy choice. In the 1980s, US policy makers and regulators reversed their long tradition of protecting and encouraging local ownership of the banking system. For different reasons—including the rise of political ideology opposed to any government regulation—they began instituting a series of sweeping legislative and regulatory reforms at state and federal levels of government that paved the way for the largest banks to swallow up all those other banks. It started at the state level. In 1980, Maine was the only state that allowed corporations based out of state to acquire banks within its borders. By 1990, only four states still had such restrictions.[7] In 1994, Congress eliminated the last remaining federal restrictions against banks doing business across state lines. In 1999, Congress eliminated the wall between main street–oriented commercial banking and Wall Street investment banking, a division that had been put in place in response to the financial market crash that led to the Great Depression. The four biggest banks that dominate banking today—Chase, Bank of America, Wells Fargo, and Citi—were not legally allowed to exist as nationwide commercial and investment banking conglomerates until all these changes were in place by the end of the 1990s. Back in the mid-1980s, these four banks as they existed at the time only represented 6.2 percent of all banking industry assets. Now, the banking system is basically reversed from what it once was. Out of $24 trillion in assets across the entire US banking industry in 2024, these four biggest banks hold $9.4 trillion, or 39 percent of banking industry assets—the same exact share of the industry that community banks once held.[8]

Some would say the shift toward bigger banks is for the better, including many in the banking industry. Bigger banks, the argument goes, are more convenient for consumers and businesses, offering larger branch networks, more ATM locations, and economies of scale that lower costs. Larger-scale banks can squeeze more investment into creating more user-friendly technology, including online and mobile banking, as well as promising more efficient underwriting and loan approvals. They say bigger banks are more stable and more capable of weathering economic shocks, but when the whole economy goes through a rough time, the government has had to bail out banks of all sizes. In earlier periods of US history, the Federal Reserve system, federal deposit insurance, and the Federal Home Loan Banks were all originally created to protect and support banks of all sizes, including the smallest community banks. By the time of the global financial crisis, the federal government's new approach was clear: it chose to bail out big banks over community banks, even though big banks had more to do with causing the crisis in the first place.

No matter what the big four banks say about their intentions—and there are some very well-intentioned people doing some very interesting community-oriented work at those big four banks—the actions of the big four banks overall show that they're just not as interested as community banks in making investments in communities. Out of the $2.7 trillion in the combined investment portfolios of the 4,128 community banks, $1.9 trillion or 70 percent of community bank portfolios are actual loans to people or businesses, nonprofit organizations, or government bodies.[9] Meanwhile, out of the $9.5 trillion in the combined portfolios of the big four banks, $3.9 trillion or just 41 percent of their portfolios are actual loans. The more these biggest banks come to dominate the banking system, the less invested the whole banking system is in the places we work, produce, play, shop, and call home.

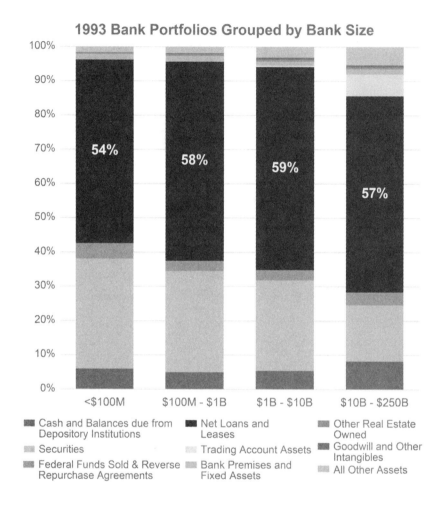

1993 Bank Portfolios Grouped by Bank Size

Legend:
- Cash and Balances due from Depository Institutions
- Net Loans and Leases
- Other Real Estate Owned
- Securities
- Trading Account Assets
- Goodwill and Other Intangibles
- Federal Funds Sold & Reverse Repurchase Agreements
- Bank Premises and Fixed Assets
- All Other Assets

In 1993, when all banks including the biggest banks were still subject to significant geographic restrictions, the whole US banking system was primarily invested in loans, as shown by the percentages displayed above corresponding to "net loans and leases" in bank portfolios. In 1993, there were no banks larger than $250 billion in assets. (Data source: Federal Financial Institutions Examination Council Call Report Data)

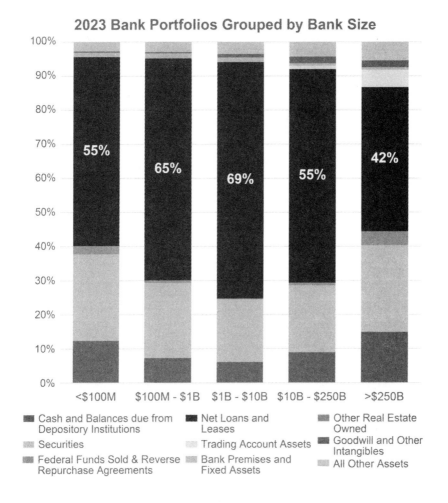

2023 Bank Portfolios Grouped by Bank Size

The difference thirty years makes. By 2023, the geographic restrictions were long gone, as were restrictions between main street–focused commercial banks and Wall Street–focused investment banks, and there was an increasing number of large banks above the $250 billion asset threshold. (Data source: Federal Financial Institutions Examination Council Call Report Data)

The differences are even more apparent when you drill down into the kinds of loans that each group of banks make. Community banks have $1.4 trillion in real estate loans in their portfolios—loans made for the purposes of building, acquiring, or maintaining homes, apartment buildings, shopping centers and other commercial buildings, industrial buildings, or farmland. The big four banks combined are more than three times the size of all 4,128 community banks combined, yet the big four have just the same amount invested in real estate, $1.4 trillion.

You can also see important differences when it comes to small businesses, the lifeblood of so many neighborhoods, not just because they make places more vibrant, but also because small businesses employ close to half of all workers and account for two-thirds of all new jobs in any given year.[10] Community banks have $223 billion in small business loans in their portfolios, whereas the big four banks have just $110 billion invested in small businesses.[11] That comes as no surprise to most small business owners, who rank small banks highest in terms of borrower satisfaction every year in the annual Small Business Credit Survey conducted by the Federal Reserve system.[12]

Some back-of-the-napkin calculations hint at what things might be like if community banks were still as prevalent as they once were.[13] Assuming that community banks would have roughly the same distribution of lending and other investments as they do now, only they were 39 percent instead of 11 percent of the banking system, community banks would have $3.2 trillion more invested in real estate loans. Those are loans that could be helping to build or maintain all the housing we need at prices that average- to low-income households can actually afford or loans to rehab and revitalize downtowns or main streets that have otherwise been struggling for years, even before the COVID-19 pandemic hit. Community banks would also have $513 billion more invested in small business loans if they still represented the same percentage of the banking industry today as they did in 1984. Many of those hypothetical small business loans could be loans to Black or Hispanic small business owners, whom today are still twice as likely to be denied small business loans compared to their non-Hispanic White counterparts.[14] Some of those hypothetical loans could be for the installation of solar power arrays on the roofs or over the parking lots of every hotel, grocery store, shopping center, warehouse, barn, condo, or apartment building across the United States.

I could pepper you with even more numbers about all the badly needed investments that communities need—from investments in affordable housing to small businesses or economic development, renewable energy, infrastructure, and more. But chances are that you might already have some ideas about the investments your community needs and has probably needed for a long time by now. Don't get me wrong—the consolidation of the banking sector isn't the only reason your community isn't getting the investments it needs. Political will, zoning, explicit and implicit racism, sexism, and xenophobia all contribute to the systemic barriers that hold some communities back and not others. Based on my reporting as a journalist over the past decade, what I've learned and gathered in this book are stories showing that as part of making those changes that we want to make in our communities, nobody has to wait for big banks to swoop in and save us, nor should anyone have to protest or beg big banks to do things they just aren't set up to do. The banking system can be much more locally owned and locally controlled. It has been before, and the results speak for themselves.

Before the 1980s, when US policy makers protected and encouraged locally owned and locally controlled banking institutions, including traditional community banks as well as alternatives like credit unions and savings and loan associations. Those community banking institutions were as crucial to building the United States as canals, railroads, automobiles, or unions. Cities, towns, and counties across the growing country clamored to have their own banks, and it was often cause for celebration if they got them. Between 1821 and 1835, the New York State Assembly received 563 petitions for bank charters from 111 cities and towns.[15] It was far from a perfect process—back in those days, obtaining a bank charter required going directly to state elected officials, opening up opportunities for corruption, bribery, and kickbacks. Only 45 petitioners from 40 municipalities across New York State obtained a bank charter during those years. Regardless of some shady dealings behind some of those banks, the newly chartered institutions went out and financed new industries and new infrastructure, including new housing for workers and their families, and filled bustling main streets with local businesses. By

1870, municipalities in New York that got a new bank between 1821 and 1835 were roughly twice the population of comparable municipalities that had not obtained a bank.[16] As the country grew and expanded westward, community banking helped lead the way, financing farms, homes, businesses, and infrastructure. We can't ignore, however, that it all was built on stolen land, much of it was cultivated using stolen labor, and for most of that history, nearly all banks made every intention to limit or avoid doing business with anyone besides White men.

We can't simply go back to the way things were before the 1980s. Nearly all those thousands of community banks that once existed across the United States, as well as many of the thousands that remain, were at one time or another guilty of redlining—the practice of denying loans to individuals or entire neighborhoods on the basis of race, ethnicity, or national origin. For decades, redlining wasn't just allowed, it was codified as a lending practice under federal housing policies that helped create wealth through homeownership for millions of White families while denying those same opportunities to Black, Hispanic, Asian, Indigenous, and other people of color. The rules under those policies incentivized banks to make loans in areas deemed safe for lending—which happened to be White neighborhoods, whose residents and leaders found all kinds of formal and informal ways to keep out people of color—while also excluding Black, Latino, and largely immigrant neighborhoods from access to those same incentives. Thus, even where people of color created their own banks to serve their own communities, federal housing policies locked out those banks from offering the same level of support that White-owned community banks could provide to White communities. It was a case of separate and unequal, by law. Even though redlining is now outlawed, it still happens as a matter of practice, and banks of all sizes still get caught and penalized for it. Redlining has been a major factor contributing to persistent racial wealth gaps in the United States, where the median net worth of White households in 2022 was $285,000, compared to just $44,900 for Black households and $61,600 for Hispanic households.[17]

Since 2015, I've been reporting on efforts to support economic justice in those neighborhoods that most banks, both big and small, have historically excluded. The people in these communities still have many valid reasons for remaining skeptical about banks. Politicians from both sides of the aisle and from all races have a history of celebrating and promoting banks owned by people of color as a way to distract from their unwillingness to make broader changes that are necessary to undo generations of systematic, race-based exclusion and disinvestment.[18] Even after the Fair Housing Act of 1968 outlawed redlining, early waves of new federally subsidized lending in communities of color were predatory and deceptive in nature, undermining Black homeownership rather than supporting it—what race scholar Keeanga-Yamahtta Taylor dubbed "predatory inclusion."[19] Anyone interested in community banking has to acknowledge these harmful histories and patterns if there's any hope to avoid repeating them in the future.

At the same time, through my reporting over the past few years, I've encountered banking institutions in city after city rooted in these same historically redlined communities that offer examples for others to emulate, build upon, and learn from. They're all, in different ways, exceptions to the rules of racism, sexism, xenophobia, and other -isms and phobias that have plagued—and continue to plague—many community banks. They make the case that communities that aren't getting access to credit from others deserve the chance to have their own locally owned and locally controlled banking institutions. I've also come across institutions created with specific missions around community development in historically redlined areas or that have missions to invest in clean energy and energy efficiency or more environmentally sustainable food systems. They illustrate how locally owned and locally controlled banking institutions have an irreplaceable role to play in making these critical, long-overdue investments. In addition to community banks proper, they include credit unions and community loan funds that have emerged as alternative models for providing access to credit when and where communities believe that other models just won't suit their purposes. Even if they aren't formally banks or credit unions just yet, all these efforts deserve to have that status and all the powers and benefits that go along with it—like the ability to hold federally insured deposits or access to the Federal Reserve. Communities deserve to have fully fledged banking institutions that won't treat them as strangers but, rather, as neighbors, friends, and family.

Starting new community banking institutions used to be much more frequent than it is today. In the decade prior to the global financial crisis, an average of 153 new banks opened their doors every year across the United States. Between 2010 and 2023, fewer than a hundred new banks opened their doors.[20]

These exceptional institutions have also taught me about the challenges and limitations they face, how they've overcome some of those challenges, and how banking regulations and policies can help them. They've also taught me that these policies sometimes prevent them from doing more of the work they have gotten really good at doing. It's not just about each community stepping up to create new community banks or credit unions to fill in gaps left by redlining or gaps in terms of investments in clean energy. These efforts need banking policies to shift the landscape back in favor of community banking.

It's important to see these community banking efforts as part of something much bigger, and much older, than some idyllic vision of America or capitalism. Like Barbara Arroyo and her colleagues at Ponce Bank, communities have been making loans to meet their own local credit needs in some way for as long as written records exist—long before capitalism and long before anyone started talking about "free markets" or "entrepreneurship." The earliest human writings discovered so far are five thousand years old from ancient Mesopotamia, and they weren't poems or letters. They were loan contracts and accounting ledgers. In those days, Sumerian temples operated like local industrial conglomerates, acquiring land, taking in donations of raw materials and livestock, and hiring farmers to cultivate crops or craftspeople to manufacture goods. Temples usually accumulated more materials than they needed, so they would sell or loan out goods to the surrounding community.[21] Villagers or merchants might borrow some grain or some livestock and then return the same items later plus an additional amount to cover interest charged—or different items but an amount of equivalent value to the total amount owed including interest. At some point, ancient Mesopotamian villagers and merchants started lending directly to each other.[22]

In medieval China, under the Tang dynasty, Buddhist monasteries operated "Inexhaustible Treasuries," taking in a never-ending stream of donations, from coinage and donated land to goods like grain, seeds, silk, cloth, and precious metals and jewels.[23] Some of it they gave to the needy, but they also lent much of it out to locals. It didn't always work smoothly. On several occasions, the Tang Imperial authorities accused monasteries of diverting grain meant for charity into high-interest loans, and the authorities would even go so far as to disband and raze thousands of monasteries at a time in retribution, wiping clean any loans on their books and redistributing goods to the needy. But they never totally wiped out or banned the practice. With inexhaustible treasuries dotting its landscape, China's economy flourished, and the Tang dynasty became a golden age of Chinese arts and culture. The inexhaustible treasuries even helped develop and operate one of the world's first systems of paper currency, which continued expanding and evolving for nearly a thousand years, outlasting the Tang dynasty and the next several thereafter.

Reclaiming community banking isn't going to fix everything. No banking system is going to end poverty, close the racial wealth gap, decarbonize the economy, or build all the housing we need at prices we can all afford. All these goals require concerted, cross-sectoral efforts to achieve. The question this book addresses is what kind of banking system is best suited to help reach all those goals. Until recently, communities across the United States have never been limited to begging big banks or wealthy philanthropists to give them access to credit. Community banking was a major component of building this country, and it very much mattered to the builders and their communities that their own financial institutions could provide at least part of the needed funding. To deny future generations that same depth of pride and not just ownership but also authorship of their community's story is to deny something at the very core of communities that human beings have built going back thousands of years. From ancient Mesopotamia to medieval China to the United States before the 1980s, community banking has been a crucial part of the human story. It has not been a perfectly rosy story, and there are many lessons to take from the past. But if the United States really wants to address its generations of race and gender-based economic exclusion and disinvestment, if it really wants to build and preserve all the housing it needs that people can actually afford, and if it wants to decarbonize that housing and all the other the buildings and infrastructure, it needs communities to take back the power of banking.

Chapter 1

For Us, by Us

Minority-Owned Community
Banks and Credit Unions

Every few minutes, the 6 train rumbles overhead along the 1700 block of Westchester Avenue in the Bronx. Beneath a bright red awning, splayed out along the sidewalk in front of a small grocery store, there's a colorful array of fresh watermelons, bananas, pineapples, oranges, strawberries, and cabbages. Clocking in at about three thousand square feet, some might classify the grocery as a large bodega.

It's been a grocery for as long as anyone alive today can remember. New York City has about two thousand small, independent neighborhood grocery stores like this one,[1] and their customers are as loyal as it gets. There are items that locals get here every week that they can't get anywhere else—definitely not at big-box stores. Across New York, these little grocery stores often reflect the immigrant makeup of their surrounding community, giving their customers a sense of belonging in the big city.

In 1968, Enrique Caro, originally from Puerto Rico, took out a $20,000 loan from Ponce Bank to acquire this single-story, two-storefront commercial property. Ponce was founded in 1960 by a group of Puerto Rican activists and business leaders in the Bronx who were fed up with existing banks, which were redlining their neighborhoods. The redlining had been happening since the 1930s, when it was largely

1

Italian immigrants in this neighborhood who were not considered to be an acceptable risk by the bankers. That opinion eventually became codified as federal policy guiding banks to avoid lending in areas "infiltrated" with "negroes," "relief families," or recent immigrants. By the 1960s, the neighborhood had become largely Puerto Rican migrants, and they experienced the same discrimination. There weren't any bankers around who knew the neighborhood, who knew who lived and shopped there, and there weren't any bankers who cared enough to get to know it. The language barrier provided another excuse.

Enrique ran the grocery store until the mid-1990s, when he retired and sold the business to a family in the neighborhood from the Dominican Republic, but he kept ownership of the building and rented the space to the new owners of the grocery. By 2004, Julio Sanchez had taken over the grocery from his brother-in-law. For years, Julio would half-joke to Enrique that one day he'd buy the building, and Enrique eventually made a promise that he would someday sell the building to Julio. Although he passed away before he could make good on that promise, Enrique's family decided to honor his wishes. They approached Julio in the fall of 2021 with an asking price for the property—$1.5 million. He had saved up some money in anticipation of this day, but not that much. Now he was worried that the family might sell the building to some speculative real estate investor who would jack up the rent and force the grocery store out of business. Julio had seen it happen before to others like him.

On the word of a friend, Julio got in touch with Barbara Arroyo at Ponce Bank. As she usually does, Barbara came out to visit the business, which is less than a mile down Westchester Avenue from her desk at Ponce Bank's headquarters, or just two quick stops on the subway. It looked like, sounded like, and smelled like the little neighborhood grocery stores Barbara had grown up around in her parent's neighborhood. Based on her assessment of this grocery's history in the neighborhood, its previous few years of cash flow, and Julio's years of success as owner-operator in an increasingly cutthroat grocery sector, Barbara was confident that Julio's little neighborhood grocery store would be able to pay back its loan for the purchase of the building, regardless of Julio's personal credit history. After all, the grocery store had been reliably paying rent all these years. Like many of the small business owners Barbara meets, Julio needed some help with his bookkeeping and tax documents, so Barbara connected him with a new accountant and worked with him to clean up some of his recordkeeping. At her previous jobs working at big banks, she wasn't given the time and flexibility to work with clients in this way, but at Ponce, it's how she spends most of her time. On July 21, 2022, Julio walked up the street to Ponce Bank's headquarters to sign the closing papers on a $1.1 million loan to buy the building he had long dreamed of owning. He's paying less now on his monthly mortgage than he had been paying in rent. For Barbara, it was just one of a dozen or so loans she closed in 2022.

Every neighborhood, every community, regardless of the race, ethnicity, or national origin of its residents, deserves to have this kind of access to credit that doesn't depend solely on credit scores or personal wealth. When they make loans, community banks in the United States have always considered broader factors like relationships, benefit to the community, potential for growth, and character—especially before the invention of credit scores in 1989. There are still thousands of community banks where bank loan officers, credit committee members, and board members make loans that depend on their relationships and their knowledge and instincts about the importance of a business in a community, like Julio's grocery store in its section of the Bronx. But Ponce is one of the very few such community banks whose ownership and leadership come from racial or ethnic minority communities.

Community banks owned and controlled by racial or ethnic minorities in the United States have always been few and far between. Legal scholar and banking reform activist Mehrsa Baradaran called the early 1930s "the golden age" of Black banking,[2] but even then only about 130 of the nearly 30,000 banks across the United States were Black-owned. Of the remaining 4,128 community banks in the United States in 2024, only 124 are classified by the Federal Deposit Insurance Corporation as a "minority depository institution"—a term that will become obsolete, as these "minority" communities will soon make up the majority of the US population. To be classified as a minority depository institution, either a majority of a bank's voting ownership must be of one designated racial minority group or the bank's board members and the bank's target market must be predominantly one or a combination of minority groups. Among minority depository institutions today, 22 community banks are classified as Black, 22 as Hispanic, 19 as Native American, and 56 as Asian and Pacific Islander.[3]

While it's much more likely today than it was in past decades for non-Hispanic White-owned community banks to do business with people of other races and ethnicities, recent research reveals the ongoing starkness of the divide. Banks still tend to locate their branches in neighborhoods whose residents look like the banks' leadership or ownership, according to a joint analysis by researchers at Johns Hopkins University and the National Bankers Association, a national trade association for minority-depository institutions.[4] Non-Hispanic White-owned banks tend to locate their branches in predominantly non-Hispanic White zip codes, whereas Black minority depository institutions tend to locate branches in predominantly Black zip codes, Hispanic institutions in Hispanic zip codes, and so on. A follow-up study from the National Bankers Association found that minority-designated banks or credit unions far outperformed their nonminority counterparts in terms of lending to majority-minority census tracts.[5] Another pair of researchers, using publicly available residential mortgage data, found that almost 70 percent of mortgages from minority-depository institutions go to borrowers of the same race as the owners of the bank, and minority borrowers applying for mortgages at banks whose owners are of the same minority group are 9 percent more likely to be approved than otherwise identical minority borrowers in nonminority banks.[6] On the small business front, small businesses owned by people of color are just half as likely as White-owned small businesses to be fully approved for a loan, line of credit, or cash advance at a small bank[7]—a disparity that starts to make sense when you consider that community banks remain an important source of credit for small businesses, yet there are so many more community banks owned by or serving White communities.

It's hard to say how many community banks or credit unions should be designated as minority banks or credit unions, but their numbers today are far behind their shares of the population overall. The US Census Bureau's 2024 estimates say 42 percent of US residents identify as Hispanic or non-White.[8] If the percentage were the same for community banks and credit unions, there would be 1,739 community banks designated as minority depository institutions (compared to 124 in reality) and about 2,000 credit unions with a minority designation (compared to 492 in reality).

The race and ethnicity of a bank's ownership and leadership still shape where a bank does business and with whom. Race and ethnicity shape the imaginations of loan officers and credit committees when it comes time to make a judgment call on whether a particular business or real estate project is likely to succeed and repay a loan. For all the numbers that bankers like to see before approving a loan, many lending decisions still come down to someone getting the benefit of the doubt, and in the United States today, it's still more likely someone gets the benefit of a doubt when they look like the person or people making the decision on a loan. Across the entire United States, there are still 4,004 non-Hispanic White-owned community banks whose loan officers and credit committees are giving that benefit of the doubt to those who look like their ownership and leadership, whereas just 124 minority-designated community banks are doing the same for those who look like their ownership and leadership. Ponce Bank is the only Hispanic minority depository institution based in New York City, a city where 2.4 million of its 8.3 million residents are Hispanic. There's only one Black minority depository institution based in New York, despite the city having 1.9 million Black residents. Meanwhile, New York City is home to 20 non-Hispanic White-owned community banks for a city with 2.6 million non-Hispanic White residents. In Baltimore, a metro that is 40 percent Black, there are 13 community banks, but only one is a minority depository institution, the Black-owned Harbor Bank of Maryland. In New Orleans, a metro that's 49 percent people of color, out of ten community banks, the only minority depository institution is the Black-owned Liberty Bank and Trust.

Headwinds

The lack of banks created by and for communities of color in the United States is a product of design and history. By design, each community that wants a bank has to come up with its own startup capital for the bank.

Historically, it might be one successful merchant or builder or a group of previously successful business owners who would pool the wealth they had accumulated to provide startup capital for a bank, or a bank's founders might raise startup capital from their previous business connections. It didn't take an exorbitant amount of wealth to start a bank, but in the country's early decades, the vast majority of Black people in the United States were still violently enslaved and denied any opportunity to build up wealth for themselves. After the Civil War, Jim Crow laws relegated most Black workers to low-wage sectors like sharecropping or domestic work, hampering the ability of recently emancipated Black communities to accumulate enough wealth to start their own banks.

When it came to the potential for new banks to form among recently emancipated Black communities, the rise and fall of Freedmen's Bank did as much if not more damage than good. Congress chartered Freedmen's Bank in 1865 as part of a package of post–Civil War reconstruction efforts. The package initially included land granted to recently emancipated families, as well as a wide range of social programs, but in its final form, the bank was really all that remained. One of the bank's immediate goals was to provide a place for Black soldiers who had fought for the Union Army to deposit their wages, which for many of them was the first time they'd ever been paid for their labor. Initially, the bank was a success, opening accounts for recently freed slaves, Black soldiers in the Union Army, Black churches, Black mutual aid societies, Black business owners, and even Howard University. Because its charter came direct from Congress, it was allowed to open branches in multiple states, unlike other banks at the time, which were constrained to doing business only within the state where they were originally chartered or headquartered. The congressional charter also gave customers the impression that the bank was implicitly guaranteed by the federal government, even though that wasn't actually the case. From 1865 to 1872, Freedman's Bank opened thirty-seven branches in seventeen states and the District of Columbia, and nearly $4 million (equivalent to $100 million today) was deposited in the bank by an estimated 100,000 individuals, the majority of whom were Black.[9] Freedmen's Bank also became known for hiring Black people as tellers and other branch-level staff and management, which helped instill trust in the bank from Black communities while also imbuing knowledge in those communities about the day-to-day operations of a bank.

But Freedmen's Bank was structurally limited in its ability to make actual investments in Black communities. At first, the bank's charter only allowed the bank to invest in government securities, meaning that it couldn't make loans to Black people and businesses who held their deposits in the bank. Although Freedman's Bank had hired many Black staff at the branch level, it was never actually owned by Black people, and its senior leadership and board of trustees were primarily White men. In 1870, the bank's trustees convinced Congress to amend the charter of Freedmen's Bank to allow for real estate lending, which the all-White executives of Freedmen's Bank promptly directed into speculative railroad and other real estate projects led by their friends and associates. Although 92 percent of Freedmen's Bank depositors were Black, 80 percent of the bank's loan dollars went to White borrowers who were often part of the bank trustees' business networks.[10] Almost all the loans actually violated the criteria for lending in the bank's charter, and more than 95 percent of delinquent loans were never paid, which suggests that the borrowers took out the loans knowing that there's a good chance they wouldn't ever have to repay them.[11] Desperate to maintain the bank's reputation, the trustees hired abolitionist icon Frederick Douglass as chief executive officer of the bank in March 1874. Douglass was unaware of the state of the bank's portfolio until after he took the position, and it didn't take him long to recommend shutting it down, which it did in June 1874. At the time, 61,131 remaining depositors still held nearly $3 million in deposits at the bank. Only 20 cents of every dollar owed to those depositors was ever returned to them.[12] The whole debacle sowed a deep suspicion of banks among Black communities, which hampered the creation and growth of their own banks well into the twentieth century (some would say even into the twenty-first).

Facing all those headwinds, the first actual Black-owned bank in the United States didn't come onto the scene until 1888, when the United Order of True Reformers, a mutual aid group founded by formerly enslaved individuals in Richmond, Virginia, obtained a state bank charter. Following in those footsteps, by 1920 five other Black-owned banks had opened their doors in Richmond, including St. Luke Penny Savings Bank.

Maggie

The daughter of an ex-slave and a White confederate soldier, Maggie Lena Walker (neé Draper) was born in Richmond on July 15, 1864. After the Civil War, during Reconstruction, Maggie was among the first Black children to attend public schools in Richmond's segregated public school system. When she was eleven years old, her stepfather died, and she started helping out with her mother's laundromat. Three years later, as a teenager, she became a member of the Independent Order of St. Luke, another mutual aid group founded by former slaves. Maggie eventually rose to become head of the Independent Order of St. Luke in 1899. At that moment, the organization was in danger of folding, with only a thousand members across fifty-seven chapters, $31.61 in its coffers, and $400 in debt to its name.[13] In 1901, Maggie gave a speech outlining her vision for revitalizing the order, which included establishing the order's own department store, a factory, a newspaper, and a bank. Following the model laid out by the True Reformers, Maggie raised the startup capital for St. Luke Penny Savings Bank from the members of her order, selling them $1,247 in ownership shares of the bank, an amount equivalent to $43,210 in 2023 dollars. On November 2, 1903, St. Luke Penny Savings Bank opened its doors on the first floor of the order's new headquarters in Richmond's historic Jackson Ward, making Maggie the first woman of any race in the United States to charter and serve as chief executive of a bank. On its first day in business, the bank opened 280 accounts holding $8,000 in deposits, equivalent to $279,137 in 2023 dollars. Although some account holders deposited hundreds of dollars, some deposited only a few.[14] The minimum deposit to open an account was $1.

St. Luke Penny Savings Bank became known early on for its unconventional lending practices, created to meet the needs of Black households living under the South's oppressive Jim Crow laws enforcing racial segregation. It would make loans as small as $5. Unlike most banks, which required 50 percent down payments for home loans with five-year maturities, St. Luke Penny Savings Bank accepted down payments as low as 10 percent. Typically, when loans reached maturity, banks expected borrowers to make a huge lump sum payment for the remaining balance on the loan, often forcing families to sell their home to make that payment. Maggie's bank instead allowed families to refinance into a new loan, keeping them in the homes that were so hard for Black families to come by during the era of Jim Crow. The bank also relied on ad hoc credit committees that included members of the community as part of approving loans. It also made heavy use of asking borrowers to have one or more cosigners who could vouch for their character—and would be on the hook to repay the loan in case the borrower couldn't. When the Great Depression hit, Maggie's bank merged with two other struggling Black-owned banks in Richmond to preserve their customers' ties to a Black-owned bank, in the process changing its name to Consolidated Bank and Trust.

The racial wealth gap doesn't just explain why it's rarer for communities of color to start their own banks. It also helps explain why it's always been harder for these banks to survive. Consolidated Bank and Trust held the status of being the longest running independent Black-owned bank until 2005. The bank had been through some tough years, and it was under pressure from regulators to come up with a plan to raise additional capital from shareholders to avoid failure. In those situations, White-owned community banks may raise additional capital from family or others in the bank owners' social circles. The legacy of racial wealth disparities means that Black-owned community banks have much less capital to tap into from their ownership's networks. Facing those limitations, Consolidated Bank and Trust merged in 2005 with a nonminority bank, keeping its accounts open but ending its run as a minority depository institution. It would be a foreshadowing of what was to come as a consequence of the subprime mortgage crisis and Great Recession, which hit all banks hard—even if they weren't engaged in subprime lending. As of 2008, there were still 186 community banks classified as minority depository institutions (40 of which were Black institutions). By 2020, there were just 120 community banks classified as minority depository institutions (20 of which were Black).

A Mutually Beneficial Option

Regardless of race or ethnicity, in situations where a community may not have enough wealth to start a traditional commercial bank, alternative models have historically emerged as a solution for providing access to credit and basic financial services. Mutual banks were among the earliest of those alternatives. Unlike traditional banks, mutual banks don't have shareholders who purchase ownership shares in the bank and share in any profits that the bank might pay out at the end of every quarter. Instead, mutual banks are "owned" or controlled by their depositors, all of whom are invited to participate (but not necessarily vote) in the selection of board members who oversee and help run a mutual bank. Ponce Bank was originally chartered as a mutual bank in 1960, although it converted into a conventional ownership structure in 2021 (we'll come back to how and why that happened later in this chapter). Many minority depository institutions were originally chartered as mutual banks, including Carver Federal Savings Bank, the only Black minority bank headquartered in New York City.

Also known as savings and loan associations or building and loan associations (Ponce Bank was founded as Ponce de Leon Federal Savings and Loan Association), mutual banks historically started out with a social purpose in mind, although they've sometimes fallen short of their original intentions. Mutual banks were immortalized in Frank Capra's 1946 film *It's a Wonderful Life* starring Jimmy Stewart as George Bailey, who reluctantly took over Bailey Brothers Building and Loan, the fictional mutual bank George's father had started. The real story of mutual banks in the United States begins in 1816,[15] when the Philadelphia Savings Fund Society became the country's first mutual bank to receive deposits, followed the next year by Boston's Provident Institution for Savings. At that time, even though mainstream commercial banks were almost all locally owned, they often limited their services to business owners and wealthy families. Mutual banks started out as a way for working-class households—often recent immigrants—to pool their savings and earn a modest amount of interest while investing in one another's homes and businesses. They were clustered in the northeast United States because during the nineteenth and early twentieth centuries, when mutual banks became popular, the Northeast was the country's most populous region, with new immigrants constantly coming from Europe in waves. By 1914, mutual banks held a majority of deposits across the six New England states, including 76 percent of deposits in New Hampshire, 70 percent in Connecticut, and 53 percent in Massachusetts.[16] In 1914, out of 640 mutual banks across the entire United States, 597 were in New England, New York, New Jersey, and Pennsylvania.[17] Today there are still 426 mutual banks, about half of them in the Northeast, with some in the Midwest concentrated in Ohio and Illinois.[18]

Nearly all mutual banks are also considered community banks, focusing on very specific metropolitan areas or rural counties, although some mutual banks are larger in size and scope. One infamous former mutual bank, Washington Mutual, grew so large that its failure helped spark the global financial crisis of 2007–2009. But most mutual banks are smaller, in part because they don't have profit-motivated shareholders who pressure leadership to keep profits growing every quarter.

For a mutual bank like Ponce, instead of getting startup capital from founders who buy ownership shares in the new bank, the founders each pledge to deposit a certain amount of money that they cannot withdraw from the bank for a set period of time. Unlike most bank deposits, pledged deposits are not covered by deposit insurance from the Federal Deposit Insurance Corporation. In lieu of startup capital from shareholders, the pledged deposits temporarily serve as a new mutual bank's regulatory capital—that's the dollar amount bank regulators require banks to set aside as a cushion against losses. The required amount is based on a proportion of a bank's overall assets. The minimum required ratio of regulatory capital is 8 percent, or roughly $1 of regulatory capital for every $12 in loans and other investments in the bank's portfolio. After several years, because they don't have to pay profits to shareholders, a successful mutual bank can pile up enough in retained profits that it can use those funds to replace pledged deposits as its regulatory capital. Unlike conventional stocks, pledged deposits don't go up in price. So, by the time a mutual bank has repaid its founders' pledged deposits, the founders have only gotten back what they put in, dollar for dollar, leaving the bank with no formal shareholders or owners. Instead, mutual banks are controlled by their depositors, who participate in the selection of the mutual bank's board of directors and may get to vote directly on certain major business decisions, similar to a credit union.

Ponce Bank's founders were rallied together by Enrique Campos Del Toro, a former attorney general of Puerto Rico. He'd previously established a mutual bank in Puerto Rico, called First Federal Savings and Loan.[19] Upon learning of the plight of Puerto Rican migrants in New York, particularly in the historically redlined Bronx, he set out to find allies to help establish a new mutual bank to serve their community. Ponce's first board chair was Antonio Acosta Velarde, a physician who in the same year of Ponce Bank's founding was appointed to a new advisory board established by the mayor of New York City to help implement an expansion of the city's public assistance programs.[20] For many years, the South Bronx had its own George Bailey: Erasto Torres, long-time former CEO of Ponce Bank. The bank's founding board members recruited him from their beloved Puerto Rico to come and run Ponce Bank in 1961, and his tenure as CEO lasted until 2011. He passed away in 2013, but the bank he left behind remained Bailey-like, specializing in real estate lending for smaller landlords or small businesses like the grocery store that Julio Sanchez owns today. Ponce also grew beyond the South Bronx to serve growing Hispanic communities across the rest of the New York area. Erasto was known for maintaining long friendships with the bank's clients, like Cuban immigrant Jose Perez, who started out in the 1970s with just one shoe store and—with the bank's funding— eventually grew to ten locations across New York and New Jersey. Erasto and Jose would regularly meet for lunch on Arthur Avenue, the Bronx's famous Little Italy. Jose would bring along his son, James, encouraging him just to sit and listen. Once he was old enough, James would eventually open his first bank account at Ponce. James took over the businesses after his father passed away unexpectedly in 2000. Ponce Bank continued to invest in the Perez family's business, Josmo Shoes, which expanded into wholesale and now also includes several warehouses in New Jersey. In 2022, thirty-two years after James opened his first bank account at Ponce, the bank invited him to join its board—which still meets every Thursday to review the bank's recent activity and finances. Being a board member was much more intense and time consuming than James expected, but it's helped him come to appreciate the amount of time and effort it takes to provide access to credit for people and communities that other institutions aren't interested in serving.

As of December 2023, Ponce Bank had $2.7 billion in assets, of which $1.9 billion were loans—a ratio of 70 percent. That's actually on the low side for Ponce, due in part to currently high interest rates, conditions set by the Federal Reserve as a way to combat high inflation by discouraging people and businesses from taking out new loans. In previous years, Ponce's loans have made up as much as 85 to 90 percent of its portfolio. Nearly all its lending is in real estate, which is typical for a bank that historically started out as a mutual bank. Its top lending category was multifamily residential—apartment buildings with at least five units, the kinds of buildings where most New Yorkers live.[21] Another big segment of Ponce's lending is in single-family housing, concentrated in New York City's outer boroughs of Queens, Brooklyn, and the Bronx.[22] Meanwhile, commercial real estate loans like the one Julio took out for his grocery store were about $310 million of Ponce's portfolio as of 2023.

Another way to gauge a bank's connection to the community is its deposit base. How many accounts does the bank have, and what's the average amount in those accounts? As of December 2023, Ponce Bank had about 46,000 open accounts holding $1.5 billion in deposits, an average of $33,300 per account. About 98 percent of those accounts held less than $250,000—and if you just count accounts holding less than $250,000, the average per account is just $19,000, most of which is in savings accounts. Out of $1.5 billion in total deposits at Ponce, $1.2 billion is in savings accounts, certificates of deposit, money market accounts, or other similar kinds of limited-access accounts that aren't used for typical day-to-day transactions. In its disclosure documents to investors, Ponce describes its primary deposit base as "a large and stable base of locally employed blue-collar workers with low-to-medium income, middle-aged, and with limited investment funds. Within the base of locally employed blue-collar workers there is a significant, and growing, portion of recently immigrated, younger, lower-skilled laborers."[23]

Ponce Bank today is no longer a mutual bank. In 2021, it completed the long process for a mutual bank to "go public," meaning that it is now a publicly traded company. To go public, a mutual bank's depositors first have to vote on doing so, with a majority required to approve the change. Then the mutual bank's existing depositors have first dibs on buying new ownership shares in the bank—essentially, they have an opportunity to turn some of their deposits into conventional ownership shares that they can later sell to other investors on the stock market. In

2017, on the eve of the bank going public, depositors held $707 million in their accounts at Ponce. Existing depositors of Ponce Bank ended up buying all the ownership shares in the bank's initial public offering. By the end of the process in 2021, Ponce depositors had invested a total of $218 million into their bank. As a publicly traded company, Ponce Bank retained its status as a minority depository institution since a majority of its board members are Hispanic and its customers in New York City are predominantly Hispanic.

Going public was not an easy decision for Ponce's leadership. There's a risk now that some larger bank or Wall Street firm eventually buys up enough shares from smaller shareholders that it can take control of the bank and start influencing it to act more like a mainstream commercial bank. The benefit of raising $218 million from Ponce selling itself to its depositors is that those dollars have helped ensure that the bank can compete with mainstream banks that are now opening up branches and taking in deposits from neighborhoods they were ignoring back when Ponce Bank was founded. Although big banks might be taking those deposits, there are still loans to be made in these places that big banks either can't make or don't want to make. Ponce Bank today continues to find borrowers who otherwise would be left out, like Julio and his grocery store, making sure that at least some of the deposits from these communities support investments that benefit these communities in terms of businesses that serve them or buildings where they can afford to live. Even though there's a risk to going public, Ponce wouldn't have been able to reach as many new borrowers without the regulatory capital raised from doing so. Since 2017, Ponce Bank has more than tripled in size, although it is still ranked just seventieth in terms of market share of deposits in the New York City metropolitan area.

The Cooperative Alternative

Rachel Macarthy is not your typical CEO of a community banking institution. One day in 2022, a long-standing account holder came into her bank looking for a personal loan. Rachel recalled that he'd paid off a previous loan and had also benefited from a program to skip a payment on that loan during the COVID-19 pandemic. But she also knew that he had a DJ business, and in a conversation with him about this new loan, she found out that he was looking for funding to buy some new DJ equipment. He hadn't heard yet that Rachel's institution had recently launched a small business lending program, which meant if he applied for a small business loan instead of a personal loan, he could qualify for a larger amount based on his business plan and prior track record. He still needed to incorporate a limited liability company for his DJ business, but Rachel was more than happy to help him through that process so that he could get all the capital he really needed.

Days like that are becoming more frequent for Rachel, the CEO of New Covenant Dominion Credit Union. It's based in the Bronx, right in Ponce Bank's backyard. But the Bronx is a big place, and there's no reason Ponce Bank or any other bank has to have a monopoly on every single dollar of deposits or loans in the Bronx or across New York City. If a community can prove that it has enough unmet credit needs, even in Ponce's own backyard, there are different models for that community to try to meet those needs, including conventional community banks, mutual banks, or, in this case, a credit union. Chartered in 2007, New Covenant Dominion Credit Union also comes out of the long tradition of faith-based institutions starting credit unions as part of their broader ministry or community work.

The first credit union in the United States was St. Mary's Cooperative Credit Association, which opened for business on April 6, 1909, in Manchester, New Hampshire. Its organizers established the credit union to serve French-speaking immigrant textile mill workers whom banks were excluding at the time. One of the organizers was the pastor of a local Catholic church, and a local attorney offered his own home to house the credit union initially. Credit unions differ from banks in that they are structured as not-for-profit member-owned cooperatives, meaning that regardless of how much a member might have saved up in the bank, each member has just one vote over key decisions such as electing the credit union's board of directors. A credit union's members come from potential membership bodies—what credit unions call their "field of membership"—such as workers at the same company along with their families, members of a faith-based congregation or an association of some kind like a Rotary Club, or residents of a specific geographic area. As not-for-profit enterprises, credit unions are exempt from federal taxes, and credit union board members are all volunteers—unlike conventional or mutual bank board members, who typically get a stipend for their time spent in board meetings or committee meetings.

Similar to community banks, credit unions used to be much more numerous than they are now. There were 15,412 credit unions in 1984,[24] compared to just 4,572 credit unions by the end of 2023.[25] As credit unions have consolidated, however, they've became larger on average. The average size of a credit union in 1984 was just $9.5 million in assets,[26] whereas in 2024 the average size of a credit union ballooned to $456 million in assets.[27] Credit unions have grown so much in average size that as a group they've gained a little ground in terms of market share. In 1984, all those credit unions combined held $147 billion in assets,[28] compared with $2 trillion in assets held by all banks collectively at the time.[29] By 2024, all credit unions combined held $2 trillion in assets,[30] compared to $24 trillion in assets held by all banks.[31]

As credit unions have grown larger, some of the largest among them have started acting more like banks—and not in the good ways. According to the analysis by reporters at CNN, the largest credit union in the United States, Navy Federal Credit Union, was found to be approving home mortgage applications from White members more than 75 percent of the time while denying the same applications to Black members more than 50 percent of the time.[32] The CNN analysis found that Navy Federal Credit Union even approved a slightly higher percentage of applications from White borrowers making less than $62,000 a year than it did of Black borrowers making $140,000 a year or more. Large credit unions have also taken up other conventional bank habits, like charging predatory fees and buying naming rights to arenas, stadiums, and performance venues. In 2022, California's largest state-chartered credit union, Golden 1, took $24 million in one year of overdraft fees from its members while also under contract to pay $6 million a year for naming rights to a professional basketball stadium in Sacramento.[33]

New Covenant Dominion Credit Union nearly quadrupled in size from 2019 to 2023, but it's still a very small credit union, with just $3.4 million in assets. A majority of its members are Black or Hispanic, making it one of 135 credit unions designated as having two or more

minority groups making up a majority of their membership, according
to the National Credit Union Administration, the federal agency that
regulates credit unions and insures the deposits they hold.[34] There are
also about 260 majority-Black credit unions. That's down from 389
majority-Black credit unions in 2013, the first year that the National
Credit Union Administration's Office of Minority and Women Inclusion began producing annual reports to Congress on the numbers of
minority-designated credit unions.

Black credit unions are more numerous than credit unions with other
minority designations—just seventy credit unions are designated Hispanic, fifty designated Asian, and eleven designated Native American.
That's just over 492 credit unions—out of 4,606 credit unions overall—
that are designated under one or more minority groups. So, although
there are many more minority-designated credit unions than minority-
designated community banks, they're still strikingly rare compared to
their majority-White equivalents. That pattern also reflects historic, systemic, racial disparities in wealth. Although it takes less startup capital to
charter a credit union, raising required startup capital for a credit union
still depends on members of a community having access to some kind
of excess wealth they can donate to a credit union to use as its initial
regulatory capital, whereas community banks selling ownership shares
or mutual banks borrowing pledged deposits. As generous as communities can be, even communities of modest means, donations are always a
smaller pool of potential dollars than savings or investments.

As rare or as small as they are relative to their White counterparts,
Black credit unions have long been an underutilized resource. In a world
still full of financial institutions that make a business out of preying
on Black communities, many Black credit unions were created primarily as a way for members to have a trusted place to deposit their savings. That's especially true of the many credit unions attached to Black
churches, like New Covenant Dominion. Many majority-Black credit
unions have only part-time staff or are run by volunteers from a church
congregation. They're open for business maybe two days a week, sometimes only one day, Sunday, when members could stop by before or after
services to make deposits or withdrawals. Lending was a lower priority,
especially during the many decades when Black credit unions couldn't

access the same federal subsidies for Black neighborhoods that White credit unions could access to support home mortgage lending in White neighborhoods. On the eve of the pandemic, in December 2019, New Covenant Dominion Credit Union's loans represented just 38 percent of its assets, typical of most majority-Black credit unions across the United States. But by that moment in time, the credit union had spent several years preparing and strategizing to boost its lending, including preparations to launch a small business loan program. One of the changes was opening up the credit union's field of membership beyond members of the church to include other nearby small businesses or nonprofits and any of their employees. When the pandemic hit, the credit union was positioned to help its community through some tough years. By the end of 2023, out of its $3.4 million in assets, $2.1 million or 67 percent of New Covenant Dominion's portfolio consisted of loans. About one-third of the credit union's loan portfolio now comes from its small business loan program, including the loan for the DJ whom Rachel helped in 2022. It's been a tremendous full-circle experience for Rachel, who grew up in the neighborhood around New Covenant Dominion Church, attended the church's grade school and high school, and went on to get a business degree at Howard University. She was a founding board member of the credit union and started working in the branch as a part-time teller, moved up to loan officer, became CEO in 2021, and in 2024 was part of a team of two other credit union staff members and one volunteer from the church.

History Remains

Community banking institutions owned by or led by racial or ethnic minorities are not by themselves enough to build a more just economy for their communities. There are no such silver bullets, especially not when these communities are still denied equal access to living-wage jobs, equal access to lucrative government contracts for their businesses, equal access to public investment in everything from schools to parks to libraries to infrastructure, and more. But the ability to deploy credit within a community is an important part of a just economy that gets taken for granted, and it's about more than just the monetary value of the lending itself. For non-Hispanic White communities, locally owned, locally controlled banking institutions fueled so much of their development and in doing so helped instill a sense of empowerment and economic self-determination in those communities. White communities often feared the possibility of non-White communities gaining that same sense of economic self-determination, so much so that they often terrorized and burned down thriving Black Wall Streets—from Durham, North Carolina, to Tulsa, Oklahoma—with the full blessing of law enforcement. A generation later, White communities came with Title I Slum Clearance authority and federal funding under the guise of so-called urban renewal to ram highways and other large infrastructure projects through thriving Black communities and other communities of color, marking another wave of irreparable damage to the economic self-determination within those communities. A generation after that, mass incarceration disproportionately undermined economic self-determination in Black communities by imprisoning a huge slice of their workforce and marking those incarcerated as well as many others with the scarlet letter of criminal records. Mainstream or White-owned financial institutions by definition can't contribute to any restoration of economic self-determination within Black communities and other systemically marginalized communities. Just as White communities saw their own institutions investing and supporting them for generations, these communities deserve to have their own institutions doing the same for them.

The past and present of community banking institutions in these communities stand as evidence that there has always been an impetus within these communities to have their own financial institutions. But the stories of these institutions also illustrate the particular challenges they face when serving communities that the rest of the economy neglects or discounts by design. Disinvestment from predominantly Black, Hispanic, indigenous, or immigrant communities has led to both physical and psycho-social trauma—crumbling buildings and shattered trust—that compounds the existing systemic challenges for financial institutions serving these communities. Community banking institutions, whether community banks, mutual banks, or credit unions, are not enough by themselves to overcome all that, but they are necessary for instilling that sense of economic self-determination. To accomplish that work within the context of disinvestment and the weight of multigenerational systemic racism still surrounding them, banking institutions serving these communities need to be more than just a bank, and that's not a tagline—it's literally part of the blueprint some have already been putting into action.

Chapter 2

The Blueprint

Filling in the Gap with Intention

S hannan Herbert grew up in Montgomery County, Maryland, just outside of Washington, DC. After graduating from Howard University with a finance degree, she took a job as a junior credit analyst at a mainstream commercial bank, assessing the risk of commercial loan applications, or what banks call underwriting loans. Through an on-the-job credit training program, Shannan got to know the common underwriting refrains, like the "five Cs" of credit: character, capacity, collateral, capital, and conditions. Bankers use these criteria to assess borrowers for creditworthiness. The terms are open to interpretation, and each bank can interpret them in ways that risk perpetuating racial disparities in access to credit. "Character" can be reduced to credit scores, or anyone who can bring enough of their own "capital" to a deal can overcome weaker assessments on the other Cs. Going through her mainstream bank's credit training program, Shannan was taught, "This is policy. This is what we have to do."

Shannan progressed along a linear career path in traditional bank underwriting. Credit officers and credit departments typically stay behind the scenes, in contrast with the loan officers on the lending team who are out cultivating relationships with clients. If the lending team is made up of the bank's good cops—friendly faces to potential borrowers—the credit team is made up of the so-called bad cops, the ones who seem like their job is to find any reason to deny a loan application. They're meant to balance each other out; loan officers are supposed to advocate for their clients, whereas the credit team's job is to protect the bank's depositors and shareholders from too much risk.

Shannan went on to earn an MBA with a specialization in finance and became one of the few Black women ever to rise to the level of chief credit officer at a bank. In 2019, after she moved to a new position as chief credit officer at City First Bank, a community bank based in Washington, DC, Shannan started to peel back the layers of the underwriting onion. Under conventional underwriting guidelines for commercial real estate, banks typically only loan amounts between 60 to 70 percent of the market value of the underlying property for such projects, requiring developers to go elsewhere, perhaps to their own pockets or their friends' pockets, to come up with the rest of what they might need for a project. It's a constraint that's severely limiting if you don't have access to personal wealth or wealth from family or friends. Black households today still have just one-eighth the median wealth of White households, according to the Federal Reserve.[1]

City First was different. It was offering real estate loans up to 90 percent of the value of an underlying property, reducing the amount that developers need to come up with on their own. That's good for Black developers, cash-strapped nonprofits, and tenant-owned cooperatives who don't have a lot of their own cash to bring to the table. Loans on those terms were possible because behind the scenes it's actually two loans: one from City First Bank up to the amount acceptable under traditional bank underwriting guidelines and a second from City First Enterprises, the bank's holding company. A bank holding company is a parent company for one or more banks. Most mainstream banks, about 84 percent, are part of a bank holding company structure.[2] Some bank holding companies don't do anything by themselves; they just serve as corporate entities within the ownership structure of the bank. In other cases, they're very active on their own, maybe selling insurance or doing investment banking for clients of the bank. City First Enterprises is one of the very few bank holding companies that are nonprofits, and it makes its own loans and operates other community development programs using funds raised from philanthropic foundations, grants from public agencies, and profits from its ownership stake in the bank. Because they're affiliates, when City First Enterprises does make a loan in coordination with City First Bank, there isn't a separate application process or second set of documents to submit, making it all as streamlined as possible for the borrower. It's just one of the ways City First Bank and City First Enterprises work in tandem to make credit available to those who might not otherwise have access because of historical and ongoing discriminatory practices in conventional bank underwriting.

Shannan found it liberating to work at a bank that was structured in a way to overcome long-standing racial disparities in access to credit. While at City First, Shannan also helped launch Underwriting for Racial Justice, an initiative to connect chief credit officers at community banks, credit unions, and nonbank lenders across the United States, helping them learn from one another and spread these different loan policies and structures to even more lenders—within the group and beyond.

City First's corporate structure—and all it enables—is a product of the original intent of the founders to create a bank to serve historically redlined communities. Those founders first came together in 1993, in the basement of Foundry United Methodist Church, eight blocks north of the White House on Sixteenth Street NW in Washington, DC. It was a diverse group, largely but not entirely Black, who had come to know one another from their work in community development in and around the District. They were bankers, housing program administrators, nonprofit leaders, and affordable housing developers. Over the next five years, they incorporated the nonprofit and raised $7 million in startup capital to charter a new bank specifically with a mission to support community development in and around Washington, DC. When the bank opened its doors in 1998, the District government made the first big deposit, placing $5 million in an account at the new bank.

Fast-forward to 2022. In that year, City First Bank made $304 million in loans, of which $203 million were loans to people, projects, or businesses in low- to moderate-income neighborhoods; $173 million were loans to create or preserve nearly fifteen hundred units of affordable housing; $61 million were loans to Black-owned or Black-led businesses and nonprofit organizations; and $48 million were loans made in neighborhoods that were at least 90 percent Black.[3] City First Bank hasn't been making it all up as it went along. It has had the benefit of building on a blueprint from a bank on the South Side of Chicago where some of its founders in that church basement had previously worked, and it's not the only bank or credit union that has built on the same blueprint.

South Shore Bank

In the early 1970s, a quartet with complementary backgrounds started working together around the idea of supporting community development in neighborhoods on the South Side of Chicago that had faced redlining and other forms of racial discrimination. Two were Black— Milton Davis, a leader of Chicago's chapter of the Congress on Racial Equity, and Jim Shelton, who was working in at the Midwest regional division of the Office of Economic Opportunity, a precursor to today's US Department of Health and Human Services. Two were White— Mary Houghton, who worked at a local foundation making grants to various community groups around Chicago, and Ron Grzywynski, a computer salesman turned community bank executive.

When a White-owned community bank in the South Shore neighborhood announced plans to move its headquarters to downtown Chicago, the quartet saw an opportunity. The bank's owners had largely been ignoring or dismissing credit needs as the racial makeup of the neighborhood shifted. Chicago's Black population had been expanding as part of the Great Migration, which started in the late nineteenth century as the Black population fled the Jim Crow South for jobs in the North and West. Prior to the Great Migration, 90 percent of African Americans lived in the South, but by the time it ended in the 1970s, a majority of African Americans lived outside the South. As they arrived in cities like Chicago, real estate brokers steered them to rent properties in the redlined neighborhoods they designated for Black folks, which quickly filled up. As Black families started pushing into nearby neighborhoods like South Shore, real estate agents began using tactics like "block busting"—using racist lies such as new Black neighbors being a sign of decline and falling property values as a way to convince White

families to buy new homes in exclusively White neighborhoods or suburbs, which White families could afford because they had access to federally subsidized home mortgages.

By the early 1970s, South Shore was 85 percent Black, and the quartet believed that the bank's owners wanted to follow the White families
and businesses that had left the neighborhood. As with many significant
business decisions at a bank, moving a branch requires approval from
bank regulators. The quartet argued to bank regulators that the proposed move would violate the spirit of the laws under which the bank
had been chartered. Bank charters, they argued, mandated a bank to
serve the community where it took deposits, and if it moved its headquarters, it would no longer serve the South Shore residents who had
faithfully kept its deposits in that bank. The law was on their side at the
time, especially in Illinois, which had some of the most stringent geographic regulations on banks of any state—until the mid 1960s, banks
in Illinois were only allowed a single location. The regulators ended up
denying the application to move. The bank's owners ended up selling
the bank to the quartet's newly created bank holding company, the
Illinois Neighborhood Development Corporation, for $3.2 million—a
sum raised by selling $800,000 in shares to private investors and bor-
rowing $2.4 million from another bank.

Once they acquired the bank, known then as South Shore Bank, the
quartet set about enacting many of the ideas they'd been envisioning for
the past few years. Through their new bank holding company, South
Shore Bank's founders created a raft of affiliated subsidiaries to comple-
ment the core business of the bank. The other bank holding company
subsidiaries included a for-profit real estate company, a for-profit small
business investment fund, and a nonprofit entity that raised grant dollars
in support job-training programs, small business incubation, and other
social services that were strategically connected to the bank holding
company's overall mission. The bank started making loans to the neighborhood's predominantly Black residents to buy homes in the neighborhood or to start and grow their businesses. Some of those businesses
were contractors in commercial or residential construction and rehab,
including plumbers, carpenters, electricians, roofers, and heating and
ventilation installers. South Shore Bank identified and cultivated those

who showed potential to take on properties as local developers, starting them on smaller properties and increasing in scale as they gained experience and know-how. The job-training programs ensured that smaller "mom and pop" developers had construction workers ready to hire as they scaled up. The business incubator made sure that there were tenants to fill storefronts with businesses that served the neighborhood and kept commercial areas vibrant and crime to a minimum.

As another pillar of its strategy, South Shore Bank augmented the neighborhood's deposits with deposits from sources beyond the South Side, from those who wanted to take accumulated wealth and intentionally invest it in ways that reflected their values, including religious values. Catholic orders of nuns, specifically, were among the first to start making these kinds of deposits in South Shore Bank, eventually followed by philanthropic foundations, wealthy families, and anyone else the bank could recruit based on its mission, and they came from all over the country. It became a way for those depositors to recognize—not just symbolically, but financially—that the wealth accumulated in their name over the years was never entirely theirs and that it at least partially belonged to those who lived in neighborhoods like South Shore whom the system had long denied the opportunity to accumulate the wealth they were partially responsible for creating through their labor and creativity.

Milton Davis lived around the corner from South Shore Bank, the only member of the founding quartet who actually lived in the neighborhood (although the others lived nearby). Milton could be found walking to and from work every day carrying a scale model of the Seventy-First Street corridor the bank was using to plan neighborhood investments together with residents, business owners, and the bank's growing client base of local developers. At one end of the corridor stood the South Shore Cultural Center, formerly the clubhouse of the Whites-only South Shore Country Club, on the Lake Michigan waterfront. The country club shut down in 1974, and its liquidators eventually sold the building to the Chicago Parks District. City leaders originally planned to demolish the building, saying that "they don't need that fancy building down there."[4] South Shore Bank was part of the local coalition that rose up in protest to save the building. In the redevelopment proposal that the bank produced in 1974, it recommended revitalizing the building as a cultural and community hub for South Shore's newer, predominantly Black residents. The building still stands today and has become a popular venue for weddings, even hosting the wedding reception for Barack and Michelle Obama, the latter of whom famously grew up in South Shore. At the other end of South Shore's Seventy-First Street corridor stood South Shore Bank. It was originally a one-story building, but the bank added a second floor, moving its administrative offices upstairs so that it could rent out ground-floor storefronts at below-market rates to small businesses that came out of the bank's business incubator program. By the early 2000s, the whole corridor was still a thriving place to shop and play. It had become one of the few examples of an economically diverse, predominantly Black neighborhood, with the bank playing a key role in making it work.

After expanding to other neighborhoods on the South Side and eventually also the West Side of Chicago, South Shore Bank changed its name in 2000 to ShoreBank. It also opened affiliate offices in Detroit, Cleveland, and the Pacific Northwest, intending to replicate what it had done in South Shore to similar neighborhoods in other communities. At its peak in 2009, ShoreBank had $2.7 billion in assets, including $1.4 billion in real estate loans and $300 million in commercial and industrial loans. Even with its reliance on bringing in larger depositors from outside the community as part of its model, smaller depositors remained a significant portion of the bank's funding base. A majority of its deposits and 95 percent of its deposit accounts came from depositors holding less than $250,000 in their accounts at the bank.

ShoreBank unfortunately met a tragic end during the subprime mortgage crisis. It got hit hard, like pretty much all banks, and it needed a bailout. The nation's biggest banks got a federal bailout in the form of the federal Troubled Asset Relief Program (TARP), part of which involved the US government actually buying significant but temporary ownership shares in big banks. A very small portion of TARP was actually set aside for smaller banks and credit unions that served on low- to moderate-income communities, bailing out just eighty-four of those institutions.[5] ShoreBank was almost one of them, but at the last minute, regulators reneged on their offer to include it—probably, although it's still not clear, because of the political optics of bailing out this particular bank while there was a president in office who was so closely associated with the bank's neighborhood on the South Side of Chicago. Shore-Bank ultimately failed in August 2010.

ShoreBank's former employees still gather to mark important anniversaries, like the fiftieth anniversary of Shore Bank's founding, celebrated in August 2023. In attendance were the two living cofounders, Ron Grzywynski and Mary Houghton, along with the daughters of the late Milton Davis and Jim Shelton. The decision to leave Shore Bank out of TARP still brought up a lot of resentment and even anger among the crowd, not to mention everyone else in Chicago whose lives Shore Bank touched.

The Legacy of ShoreBank

ShoreBank's demise was but one of many contributing factors in the decline of the South Shore neighborhood's Seventy-First Street corridor. It is no longer the vibrant center of commerce and culture it once was. The surrounding neighborhood has struggled. But ShoreBank's legacy lives on through its copycats.

The first ShoreBank copycat was Southern Bancorp, based in rural Arkansas and also serving the Mississippi delta. It wasn't an exact copy. For one thing, ShoreBank's own leadership wasn't sure that the model they'd cooked up would work in a much more rural setting. More importantly, Southern Bancorp's origins weren't as rooted in a local neighborhood-based effort to fight back against disinvestment as ShoreBank was. But the Chicago community bank's reputation by the 1980s had attracted the attention of a few philanthropic foundations in Arkansas, specifically the Walton Family Foundation (as in the family that founded Walmart), and the Winthrop Rockefeller Foundation (founded by a son of oil baron John D. Rockefeller). The foundations were worried about rural areas in Arkansas and Mississippi that large banks were starting to leave behind as the banking industry was starting to consolidate. The Winthrop Rockefeller Foundation began working with ShoreBank staff to explore the possibility of a rural replication of the ShoreBank model, targeting low-income communities in Arkansas and the Mississippi delta. Bill Clinton, governor of Arkansas at the time, had also learned about ShoreBank's growing impact on the South Shore neighborhood and began his own set of conversations with ShoreBank's leadership about bringing this model to the South.

ShoreBank's leadership was also crucial to bringing in additional out-of-state support for Southern Bancorp, particularly from the Ford Foundation. With its backing from philanthropy and cheerleading from Clinton, Southern started out in a much better financial position than ShoreBank was financially back in 1973 when it first started. Instead of being on the hook for a $2.4 million loan from another bank, as Shore-Bank was, Southern started out in 1986 with $10 million in seed capital from the foundations and other wealthy investors.

In corporate structure, Southern started out almost an exact copy-cat of ShoreBank. Instead of starting a new bank, Southern Bancorp's founders created it as a bank holding company and then acquired an existing bank, thus starting out with an existing deposit base and portfolio of loans and other investments. The first bank Southern acquired was Elk Horn Bank and Trust in Arkadelphia, Arkansas, which had been in business since 1884. Following the ShoreBank blueprint, Southern Bancorp also established a set of affiliated entities through its bank holding company, including a for-profit real estate company, a venture capital fund, a small business investment fund, and a nonprofit organization. Over the decades, other banks created to serve historically red-lined communities have adapted the hybrid bank/nonprofit blueprint, including Baltimore's Harbor Bank, New York's Carver Federal Savings Bank, and City First Bank.

ShoreBank and Southern Bancorp provided inspiration for Clinton, who rose to the US presidency in 1992, to back a proposal to create the Community Development Financial Institutions Fund, the arm of the US Treasury that grants certification to Community Development Financial Institutions (CDFIs). To receive CDFI certification, financial institutions must have "a primary mission of community development" and submit data showing that at least 60 percent of their lending or investments and other services go to low- and moderate-income communities or "other targeted populations"—which include Black, Hispanic, Native, Pacific Islander, Filipino, Vietnamese, and persons with disabilities.[6] Banks, credit unions, venture capital funds, and nonbank lenders can all apply for CDFI certification, which makes them eligible for grants and other resources from the CDFI Fund itself, a growing array of state and local government funding streams for CDFIs, and an increasing number of private foundations across the United States that fund CDFIs. As of 2023, there were more than fourteen hundred certified CDFIs across the country,[7] and Shore Bank was the template for so much of what CDFIs do alongside access to capital: provide services like financial counseling, technical assistance, running business incubation programs, and providing other nonfinancial forms of support to their clients, for example. Former ShoreBank employees have gone on to work at other CDFIs in Chicago and elsewhere, including City First Bank. Many existing minority-designated banks and credit unions have also obtained CDFI certification, including both Ponce Bank and New Covenant Dominion Credit Union, and financial support from the CDFI Fund has been crucial to both of their growth stories over the past few years.

The big idea behind the CDFI Fund, which came from both Shore-Bank and from a parallel movement spearheaded by the National Federation of Community Development Credit Unions, was the recognition that locally owned, locally controlled financial institutions in historically disinvested communities couldn't simply be left to emerge and fend for themselves like equivalent institutions serving wealthier, predominantly White communities. Historic racism and other forms of discrimination mean that the communities these institutions are meant to serve don't have as much wealth they can pool together to start new community banks or credit unions, nor do they have as much individual wealth to use as collateral to obtain loans from their own financial institutions. These populations faced discrimination in job markets, leading to chronically higher unemployment rates and lower average household incomes, and by extension the local businesses serving these populations have lower average revenues and therefore need smaller loan amounts. Not to mention, there's still the burden of overcoming the long-entrenched historical headwinds against banking in historically redlined communities. The CDFI Fund was supposed to help level the playing field, supporting low- to moderate-income communities or communities of color to create their own financial institutions, providing resources to help overcome or plug in gaps that don't exist for equivalent institutions in wealthier, predominantly White communities.

But since its inception, the CDFI Fund has not led to a massive wave of new community banks of credit unions owned or controlled by communities of color or low-income communities. Some of that comes down to way it has worked in practice so far. After it was created, the CDFI Fund structured its application process to favor nonbank lenders, usually nonprofit or charitable loan funds whose staff are more accustomed to writing long grant proposals. The CDFI Fund also requires recipients to raise matching dollars from other sources, which nonprofits can obtain more easily from private philanthropic foundations—which generally don't give grants to for-profit banks or credit unions. During the CDFI Fund's first twenty years of existence, 80 percent of the funding from its main financial assistance program went to nonbank loan funds whereas just 12 percent went to credit unions and 5.6 percent went to banks, according to an analysis by Clifford Rosenthal, a historian and longtime CEO of the National Federation of Community Development Credit Unions.[8]

Factors outside the CDFI Fund's control have limited its impact over the years. Politically, it was targeted for elimination pretty much from the start. The first federal budget after it was authorized came after the 1994 midterm election in which the White House's opponents in Republican Party took over both houses of Congress for the first time since 1952. The new congressional majority was more than eager to zero-out funding for a program that had been a campaign pillar for its political enemies. The Clinton administration had originally requested $125 million for the CDFI Fund in its first appropriation, and the new Republican Congress counteroffered with $0. After President Clinton vetoed the first budget, a compromise budget passed with $50 million for the CDFI Fund's first appropriation—a far cry from the $1 billion for community development banks that Clinton had originally proposed on the campaign trail. The CDFI Fund's battles for existence continued throughout the 1990s and into the 2000s under President George W. Bush. The constant cloud of political uncertainty wasn't conducive to addressing some of the internal barriers that limited the ability of the CDFI Fund to support more new community banks and credit unions based in historically disinvested communities.

Politics also drove other changes that tilted the larger banking landscape against community banking. Clinton signed the legislation to create the CDFI Fund on September 23, 1994.[9] Ironically, one week later, he signed another bill into law that removed the last remaining federal restrictions on interstate banking,[10] opening the floodgates for today's global megabanks to swallow up thousands of smaller banks. As those megabanks grew in terms of dollars and market shares, so did their influence on policy makers who bought into the argument that bigger is better—or at least inevitable—when it comes to banking. It's a mindset that still tends to dominate today, particularly at the federal agencies that provide federal deposit insurance—the Federal Deposit Insurance Corporation for banks and the National Credit Union Administration for credit unions. Because these agencies get to approve applications for federal deposit insurance, they have de facto veto power over applications for new community banks or credit unions. They have to decide if a prospective institution's business plan is strong enough to put their agencies' deposit insurance funds at risk. When a prospective bank or credit union submits an application with a business plan focusing on a primary market that consists of one or more historically disinvested communities, it can be seen as up to two strikes against their application—one strike for proposing a smaller bank and another for serving communities that regulators may still perceive as being too risky.

A few notable examples so far—City First Bank being one of them—show what kind of impact is possible when CDFI Fund has stepped in as a source of early-stage capital for community banks and credit unions in these communities. The CDFI Fund awarded City First Bank $1.5 million in 2000, only two years after the bank had opened its doors.[11] Just two years after that, City First got another $2 million from the CDFI Fund.[12] Or there's Community Bank of the Bay, based in Oakland, California, and chartered in 1996. It was the first California organization created specifically as a federally certified CDFI. Community Bank of the Bay received $3 million over its first five years from the CDFI Fund.[13] As of the first quarter of 2024, Community Bank of the Bay had around a billion dollars in assets, including $686 million in loans, about half of that in commercial real estate.

Results

Samira Rajan was fresh out of grad school when she met the CEO of the brand-new Brooklyn Cooperative Federal Credit Union in New York on September 14, 2001. It was a deeply unsettling time. Lower Manhattan was still enveloped in a cloud of toxic smoke where the Twin Towers fell as Samira stepped out of her family's home a few miles away in Queens. Before grad school, she had worked at the Federal Reserve Bank of New York, and she was planning to go back into financial regulation and public policy. At the suggestion of a grad school professor, Samira decided to spend a year or so working with community banking institutions, getting to understand how financial policy and regulations affect people in low-income neighborhoods.

Samira found the work to be far more interesting and meaningful than she expected. By 2008, she had risen to become CEO of Brooklyn Cooperative, a position she still holds today. Meanwhile, the credit union has become arguably one of the most important economic institutions in Brooklyn, thanks to its position as one of the most prominent small business lenders in the borough of 2.5 million residents—of whom 33 percent are Black and 19 percent are Hispanic. Since 2010, Brooklyn Cooperative has made more federally guaranteed small business loans in Brooklyn than Citibank, Wells Fargo, and Bank of America combined; Brooklyn Cooperative is ranked fourth by the same measure, behind only TD Bank, Chase, and M&T Bank. In comparison to all these other banks by asset size, however, Brooklyn Cooperative is just a rounding error, with just $50 million in assets.

By promising to pay off a portion of each loan in case the borrower defaults, federal small business loan guarantee programs are meant to incentivize private lenders "to serve creditworthy small business borrowers who cannot otherwise obtain credit at reasonable terms and do not have other sources of financing,"[14] but that borrower description is broad enough to mean very different things for different lenders. Brooklyn Cooperative's federally guaranteed small business loans are much smaller than those the other banks make. It's an indicator of who it serves. A majority of Brooklyn Cooperative's members identify as Black or Hispanic. Small businesses owned by racial or ethnic minorities are typically smaller in revenue and therefore require smaller amounts of capital than those owned by non-Hispanic Whites.[15] According to data from the Small Business Administration, the federal agency that operates a few different small business loan guarantee programs, under the agency's most popular such program, the average size of a federally guaranteed small business loan within the borough of Brooklyn from TD Bank or Chase is about $125,000, while Brooklyn Cooperative averages just $24,000.

The CDFI Fund, for all its limitations and political drama over the years, was a crucial source of support to help get Brooklyn Cooperative Federal Credit Union up and running in its early days. Jack Lawson was a PhD student in economics at the New School in the late 1990s when he found a part-time job related to his research at the Ridgewood-Bushwick Senior Citizens Council (today known as RiseBoro Community Partnership). There, he began helping local businesses apply for public grants to pay for storefront improvements and other needs. Not long after Jack started, the organization began to discuss launching a credit union as part of its ever-growing suite of community development programs. Jack jumped at the chance to lead the work. It was much more in line with the economic democracy ideas he was researching.

The basics of a credit union charter application are mostly the same today as they were then. The process is also similar to the bank chartering process. It starts with a market analysis showing an unmet need in a specific area or among a specific population subgroup, like a set of employees at one company, a church congregation, a union shop, or some other kind of member-based organization. Then, similar to a bank charter application, you need a marketing plan and a business plan with growth projections based on the market analysis that show a path to financial sustainability within the first few years of operation. Also similar to a bank charter application, you have to conduct a statistically robust survey of your target market showing unmet demand for bank accounts and different types of loans from the prospective credit union. You should also have a sufficient level of deposit pledges from the community or other supporters in advance of a credit union getting final approval to open for business. In contrast with banks, whose board members receive compensation for their time, prospective credit unions need to recruit an all-volunteer board of directors and volunteer or paid initial management team, all of whom must pass credit and background checks by regulators.

All the credit union charter application work can be done on a volunteer basis, but it doesn't have to be. New York Community Trust, the local community foundation, provided early grant funding to Ridgewood-Bushwick Senior Citizens Council to support Jack's part-time salary and the other costs related to organizing a new credit union. Initially, Ridgewood-Bushwick Senior Citizens Council served as the nonprofit sponsor for the credit union, which made it easier to raise money for the credit union by tapping into the nonprofit's other frequent funders— Chase Bank, Citibank, Ridgewood Savings Bank, and other local banks and local foundations. "The relationship with the sponsoring entity was really important to opening those doors," Jack told me.

In the fall of 2000, the National Credit Union Administration approved the charter and deposit insurance application for what started out as the Bushwick Cooperative Federal Credit Union. The Ridgewood-Bushwick Senior Citizens Council provided a vacant storefront rent-free to the credit union for its first few years. The credit union severed ties with Ridgewood-Bushwick Senior Citizens Council in 2003, spinning itself off as an independent organization—thanks in part to the credit union's ability to access funding on its own from the CDFI Fund. From 2001 until Jack's departure in 2008, Brooklyn Cooperative Federal Credit Union obtained six grants from the CDFI Fund, totaling $1.1 million dollars. After Samira took over as CEO in 2008, the credit union received eight more grants from the CDFI Fund, totaling $11.3 million.

In Brooklyn Cooperative's early days, CDFI Fund grants helped cover the costs of operating the credit union while it built up its loan portfolio to the point that revenue from loan repayments could cover those costs. It wasn't easy, and it took a long time to get to that point, especially since the loans it makes are so much smaller than those made by its competitors. It really wasn't until around 2014, according to Samira, that Brooklyn Cooperative was no longer dependent on grants to cover operating costs. Grants from the CDFI Fund still play an important role in helping the credit union grow in response to the community, especially when it comes to keeping up with its required regulatory capital ratio. For credit unions, the requirement is $1 in regulatory capital for every $16 in assets.

Banks are allowed to sell shares to shareholders to raise regulatory capital, but credit unions don't have that option as member-owned financial cooperatives. A credit union's initial capital comes from donations, often raised through the church, employer, union chapter, or other member-based association that serves as the credit union's sponsor. To fund growth, credit unions either have to set aside extra earned income or can raise funds from donors, foundations, or dedicated public-sector programs like the CDFI Fund. Donations hardly ever come in as fast as deposits and new loans, so capital requirements might force a credit union to slow down approvals of loan requests or even slow down the intake of new deposits. Thanks to grants from the CDFI Fund, Samira has never had to do that.

Demand for Brooklyn Cooperative's services continues to grow every year, even in neighborhoods like Bushwick or Bedford-Stuyvesant in Brooklyn, where today it seems like mainstream bank branches pop up on every corner. There are still plenty of households in these neighborhoods that, for a variety of reasons, either can't or don't want to do business with mainstream banks, and they continue coming to institutions like Brooklyn Cooperative. On the eve of the pandemic, in March 2020, Samira's credit union held $26 million in deposits and $24 million in active loans in its portfolio. By the end of 2023, it had more than $40 million in deposits and $35 million in loans. Without grants from the CDFI Fund, the credit union would not have been able to accommodate such significant growth in such a relatively short time frame. Thanks to grant funding from the CDFI Fund, in January 2023 Brooklyn Cooperative opened its third branch, in the East New York neighborhood, where it has been growing in membership.

The CDFI Fund itself meanwhile is no longer in a constant state of political limbo. It got renewed support under the Obama administration—despite the demise of ShoreBank—and it eventually gained bipartisan support, at least in Congress. Since 2011, Congress has doled out an average of $250 million a year for the CDFI Fund, topping $300 million for the first time in 2023. Since inception, however, the fund has always received much more in funding requests than it has ever been able to fund. In the most recent round of applications for its largest single grant program, the CDFI Fund received 948 applications from organizations across the United States requesting a combined amount of $1.55 billion[16]—more than three times the amount of available funding. In 2001, when Brooklyn Cooperative first started applying for grants from the CDFI Fund, there were still only around 280 federally certified CDFIs eligible to apply. Since then, as the application process became more competitive, the CDFI Fund also prioritized applicants with prior lending track records, making it extremely difficult if not impossible nowadays for organizations to obtain CDFI Fund support in their earliest years, as Brooklyn Cooperative did.

In 2023, using part of a grant from the CDFI Fund, Brooklyn Cooperative created its own internal loan guarantee program for small business loans made to borrowers who aren't eligible for federal small business loan guarantees because the business owner doesn't have a social security number. Samira told me that with the recent influx of refugees and asylum seekers being bused into New York City from other parts of the country, Brooklyn Cooperative has been seeing dozens of them coming to join the credit union. Self-employment through a small business is often their best if not their only option to start making a living in the United States. The credit union can also help them through its own nonprofit affiliate, Grow Brooklyn, which specializes in providing free tax preparation services, including for noncitizens who sign up to pay taxes using an individual taxpayer identification number.

Brooklyn Cooperative remains an all-too-rare example of the CDFI Fund living up to its original vision of supporting historically marginalized communities to create their own full-service banking institutions that can evolve and consistently respond to their needs over time. The credit union never set an explicit goal to become one of Brooklyn's most active lenders under the federal small business loan guarantee program. Its entrée into small business lending was entirely in response to the community. Initially, as with most newly chartered credit unions, regulators only allowed Brooklyn Cooperative to start out doing small personal loans. Samira noticed early on that it was not uncommon for members to take out personal loans to support their business—bodegas, hair salons and barbershops, boutique apparel shops, and the like. Some would take out a car loan to acquire a vehicle as an independent taxicab driver or for-hire transportation provider. Except for the car loans, the credit union made most of these loans without any collateral. Most New Yorkers, including the wealthy ones, don't own a home they can put up as collateral. And, like any other deposit-taking institution, Brooklyn Cooperative is constantly on the lookout for tools to help reduce its risk. Federal small business loan guarantees became a tool for the credit union to use as a stand-in for collateral where its borrowers don't really have any. Unlike most lenders, Brooklyn Cooperative doesn't have a credit score minimum for any of its lending, including its small business lending. Its borrowers historically have had an average credit score below 650.

It's not just historically marginalized communities who need that level of connection and responsiveness from their own financial institutions. The challenge of addressing climate change is getting more critical by the day. Although there's clearly an important role for the public sector and larger financing sources to support large-scale projects to transition energy production and distribution into renewable sources, there are also plenty of smaller projects and smaller businesses that need smaller loans for smaller transactions—which community banks and credit unions are better situated to help facilitate and finance. Whether it's through newly created institutions or through existing community banks or credit unions, there's also a blueprint that communities can use as a starting point for reclaiming the power of banking to address urgent challenges related to climate change.

Chapter 3

The Greenprint

Finding Community in Values

When Nina Webster left her big bank job to work at New Resource Bank in San Francisco in 2015, she went from working on $50 million to $100 million deals to working on $100,000 to $5 million deals. But just because the deals were smaller, the work wasn't any less interesting. In fact, it became more engaging because she was working on some of the earliest deals to help smaller solar array developers scale up to meet growing demand. They were deals that other banks, even other community banks, weren't interested in—largely because they weren't familiar with the sophisticated deal structures required for setting up loan repayments and securing collateral for loans to build residential or commercial rooftop solar arrays.

Every state, and sometimes different localities in each state, has its own rules and regulations governing the relationships between the property owners where solar arrays get installed, the solar array developers and contractors who do the installing and maintenance of those arrays, and the power utilities that ultimately have to agree to purchase any power sent into the power grids that they build and maintain. In some cases, the property owner may also own the solar array. In other cases, developers lease rooftops or other surface areas from the property owner. Federal, state, or local tax credits may be involved that have to flow to whoever owns the solar array. If it's a community solar array, there may be dozens of nearby properties, businesses, or households that need their electric bills credited as subscribers for the power produced by that particular community solar array.

Today, standardized cookie-cutter deal structures work in some, although not necessarily all, solar array installation deals, but the solar industry was still in its infancy back in 2015 when Nina started at New Resource Bank. Sunrun, as of 2024 the largest US provider of solar array and power storage systems, was founded in 2007. Also based in San Francisco, Sunrun was one of those companies that got a bunch of early-stage investments from venture capital firms in the Bay Area. Back in 2015, bank executives still hadn't been able to wrap their minds around how to finance commercial and residential solar array installations on a mass-market scale. At New Resource Bank, a community bank created specifically to take on the risks of making loans that would scale up the work of environmental sustainability, Nina found herself with an unusual amount of creative leeway to figure out how to make solar lending work.

Some of the key policies to encourage residential and commercial solar installation had been in place for many years by 2015. California's net metering program was created in 1995; under net metering, utilities pay homeowners for excess solar energy they don't need that gets sent into the power grid. In California, the price paid to the homeowners is set by the California Public Utilities Commission. But the upfront cost of installation back then was too high for most homeowners to afford, even if they took out a loan. Part of the cost was the technology itself, although designs and materials have become much more cost effective over time. Another part of the cost is the scale. Like the assembly line did for cars, being able to produce and sell solar arrays in larger volumes creates economies of scale that reduce the cost per installation. In 2006, the state helped boost potential demand by creating the California Solar Initiative, a $3.4 billion, decade-long incentive program for homeowners and businesses to get rebates for installing solar arrays on their properties. Federal investment tax credits for solar also came on the scene in 2006.

All the programs and incentives increased the residential use of solar in California, but it was not quite to the tipping point. There were still pieces to figure out on the supply side, however. Who would provide the upfront financing for the solar array developers and contractors that were still mostly new businesses themselves but itching to serve the growing demand for solar array installations across the state? How would they hire more workers and purchase more equipment from solar array manufacturers while they are still waiting to get paid by their customers? Those are the gaps New Resource Bank started to bridge in the 2010s, providing loans and lines of credit to help small-scale solar developers meet the growing demand from households and businesses.

It didn't take long for other community banks and larger banks to follow. California as of 2024 was producing more solar energy from households and private businesses than any other state, and nearly 80 percent of that capacity didn't come online until after Nina first came to work at New Resource Bank in 2015.[1]

Painting Main Street Green

Peter Liu, a recovering oil industry engineer turned finance professional, never imagined that he would start a community bank. In 2004, he was working as an advisor to help craft a new strategy for California's two big state public pension funds to invest $1.5 billion in new green technologies and environmentally responsible companies. As part of that work, he talked to people in a lot of emerging sectors like solar panel installation and sustainable food production.

Much of the public pension fund's new so-called environmentally responsible investments ended up going into venture capital funds. Pension funds are always urgently in search of higher financial returns to meet their obligations to pensioners. Venture capital funds make promises of high returns using a strategy of investing in startup companies, a small percentage of which wind up making big bucks for early-stage investors, and California is home to Silicon Valley, the capital of venture capital. Peter told me that the pension funds were looking to increase their allocations to venture capital anyway. Whether or not venture capital funds actually deliver on those high returns overall as a group is a whole other story.

But in his scan of the environmentally responsible business landscape, Peter found that many of the businesses that needed capital to grow in promising sectors like solar and wind energy or organic foods weren't interested in parading in front of venture capitalists *Shark Tank* style. Many of these green-minded business owners weren't interested in establishing relationships with investors who prioritized profits over planet and people. In any case, these businesses also weren't necessarily on the path to having an initial public offering someday and getting listed on a stock exchange or being acquired by some larger multinational corporation—the typical kind of events that generate the big payday that venture capital investors eventually need to make their high returns possible. Not every business is destined to go public or get acquired in that way. The vast majority of businesses don't ever get listed on a stock exchange. Most businesses don't need venture capital investments, but they still might need affordable loans or lines of credit to secure raw materials or new tools or to bring in new employees to scale up production or open up a new product line. They need a bank.

"I thought we were missing the banking side," Peter told me. "Venture capital was very ambitious, but not something that could translate to a broad economic base. The sustainability sector needed to grow from Wall Street and Silicon Valley to Main Street."

When Peter went to some of his friends and former colleagues working in big banks and told them about what he saw as lending opportunities in environmental sustainability, nobody was interested. What Peter heard instead in response was that their big banks weren't good at entering into what they viewed at the time as new or emerging industries like clean energy or organic foods. It was too risky for them. Even if there was some familiarity with products like vegetables or dairy, they weren't interested in learning how to evaluate the financial viability of a business model that incorporated unorthodox practices like avoiding pesticides or other environmentally harmful chemicals.

Here's a secret about banks. When they say that something is too risky for them, a lot of the time it's not because there actually is too much risk. It's really because they haven't taken the time to understand how much risk there is in reality. It could be lending to a small business or an economic development project in a neighborhood they don't know very well, or it could it be lending to a business in an emerging industry they don't understand yet—like solar power installation. You might expect banks to be interested wherever there's profit to be made, and to some extent that's true. But from their perspective, why go out and learn about a new industry when there's plenty of the same old fossil fuel companies to profit from? If a bank doesn't understand how the solar panel installation industry works—who the installers are; what the latest technologies are; how much prices fluctuate on a daily, weekly, or other basis; and why those prices fluctuate—there's no way for the bank to size up how much it can loan someone to install a solar array. That bank might not care to look into a government program that mitigates some of the risk by paying off a portion of the loan via a tax credit or partially cover any potential losses on a loan in case of default.

On top of all that, if the bank doesn't understand an industry—or a neighborhood—that deeply, it can't defend itself when bank regulators come around as they do on a regular basis to monitor every bank's lending practices for safety and soundness. Unlike every other kind of lender, being regulated lenders mean that banks as well as credit unions have bank examiners coming in every twelve to eighteen months to examine their lending records and ask hard questions about loans that might seem even the slightest bit out of the ordinary, whether it's because they're made on terms that seem a little too risky or whether it's a new industry that the examiners don't know very well themselves. Bank or credit union staff to have to explain the work they've put into building their internal knowledge and building relationships that help them evaluate and take on new kinds of risks. The benefit of taking on that burden is that they can now hold federally insured deposits on their balance sheet. The ability to hold federally insured deposits is what gives banks and credit unions the ability to provide more flexible capital at lower interest rates than any other kind of lender.

Peter knew that environmentally sustainable businesses shouldn't be denied access to that kind of capital while his former fossil fuel employers had all the flexible, lowest cost capital they needed from their banks. But he soon grew frustrated that even he—someone who knew banking and finance inside and out—couldn't convince bankers of the clear opportunity to do some good for the planet while still making some money. So instead, he started asking around about how to start a new bank—a "de novo" bank in banking lingo. He reached out to Triodos Bank, a

Dutch bank that is one of the few founded with a specific social mission "to help create a society that protects and promotes the quality of life of all its members." He even reached out to ShoreBank, whose Portland, Oregon–based affiliate ShoreBank Pacific claimed the distinction as the first bank chartered specifically with a mission around environmental responsibility back when it was founded in 1997. "All [of them] told me it was very hard, but maybe California was ready for this," Peter told me.

The Chartering Process

Similar to prospective new credit unions, de novo bank applications include a market analysis showing the potential need, a business plan showing a path to financial sustainability within three years, and a marketing plan. The Federal Deposit Insurance Corporation (FDIC) and whichever bank chartering agency is involved jointly review and scrutinize everything in a de novo bank application packet.

Regulators had some skepticism about the business plan Peter submitted, although he recalls that it was not an unusual amount of skepticism. In the case of a bank failure, the FDIC potentially has to cut checks to cover the deposits it insures—up to $250,000 per depositor, per account category. That's a big incentive to set strict or conservative standards for prospective banks applying for deposit insurance. Prior to the 1980s, the agencies that issue bank charters—either state-level bank regulators or the Office of the Comptroller of the Currency at the federal level—had much more say about who got a bank charter. As part of their mandate to support economic growth and development, bank chartering agencies have an incentive to grant bank charters. Starting the 1980s, the FDIC gained more and more power over the process. By 2005, when Peter first walked into the FDIC's regional office in San Francisco, the agency effectively had veto power over bank chartering across the United States.

The entire application process took about a year, which for Peter seemed a typical amount of time for banking regulators to review an application. During this period, the regulators conduct their own independent investigation into the applicant's market analysis and the business plan. The application Peter submitted included profiles of two hundred potential customers as examples of the target market—including organic food companies, nascent solar panel installation firms, and non-profits with aligned missions like the Rainforest Action Network and former Vice President Al Gore's Climate Reality Project. The application also needs to list founding board members and the bank's initial management team, all of whom must pass a background check, including their individual financial histories, as well as go through an interview process with regulators. Other than the actual seed capital for the bank, one of the biggest startup costs is the salaries for initial management, who need to be employed by the bank even while it's still waiting for final approval to open for business.

Many applications never get beyond the initial round of scrutiny. They may never get formally submitted, or they may get withdrawn after formal submission. But if de novo bank applicants get through that initial round, they get a conditional approval from regulators. At that point, de novo banks have a standard two-year deadline to raise startup capital, unless regulators grant an extension. It wasn't that hard for Peter to raise startup capital given his industry ties and those of his fellow founding board members. To serve as the bank's founding board chair, Peter recruited Mark Finser, who had recently founded a new not-for-profit financial services firm called RSF Social Finance that became an initial shareholder of Peter's bank. Triodos Bank became an initial shareholder. There was enough buzz at the time around sustainability and clean technology that they received more investor offers than they were able to accept, Peter told me. Ultimately, after just two months of fundraising, Peter accepted offers from about two hundred initial shareholders who invested a total of $24.8 million, and New Resource Bank officially opened its doors on Howard Street in San Francisco, on September 19, 2006. Peter became vice chair. It was one of 194 new banks to open for business across the United States that year, including 15 in California.

Doubling Down on Mission

New Resource Bank had a rough first five years. From the start, it suffered from "mission drift"—under pressure to break even as quickly as possible, it initially made a lot of residential and commercial real estate loans that had little if anything to do with environmental sustainability. Besides pulling the bank away from its mission, those loans put the bank squarely in the path of the financial crisis and Great Recession that started at the end of 2007. Like most banks, however, it survived. Out of the 8,660 banks that were active at the beginning of 2007, only 564 actually failed due to the financial turmoil in 2014.[2] The total number of banks did fall to 6,500 by 2014 as a result of mergers and acquisitions.[3]

By its tenth birthday in 2016, New Resource Bank had grown to $330 million in assets in its portfolio, with $243 million or 72 percent of its portfolio in loans. More than 70 percent of its loans were made for purposes aligned with the bank's environmental sustainability mission, with the remaining 30 percent in conventional loans for commercial real estate, small business, or home mortgages.

New Resource survived the turmoil in large part by doubling down on its founding mission. During the crisis, the bank brought in a new CEO, Vincent Siciliano, who had helped save three other community banks from failure. With its new leadership in place, the bank concluded that its mission needed to be both its competitive edge in raising deposits from like-minded individuals looking for an environmentally responsible place to invest as well as its business strategy on the lending side. Coming out of the financial crisis, every loan the bank made would be mission-aligned. Leadership realized that "you can't be half-green as an institution," Vince told me. "You can't say to the world, well, we believe in certain things but then only do it half the time and continue doing traditional lending that comes out of a community bank. And that was the first big decision that, you know, in the rearview mirror may not seem so important, but at the time, it was pivotal, because it said to everyone on our board, to our employees, to our shareholders, and to the regulators, we were 100 percent committed to this mission."

It would mean saying no to some loans that might earn profits for the bank but weren't aligned with its values around people and planet. The bank came up with a questionnaire to gauge potential borrowers' inclinations toward environmental sustainability. For some prospective borrowers, it became a reason to walk away. The bank had little left to lose. If it wasn't possible to remain financially viable under its 100 percent mission constraint, the bank was already in danger of regulators shutting it down anyway. Committing to mission-driven lending felt like the only way to build, or in some cases rebuild, credibility among the bank's chosen community. It didn't necessarily mean that every business the bank made a loan to was focused on environmental sustainability. But if they were going to make that loan to a coffee shop or restaurant or bookstore, it would be made for the purpose of something related to environmental sustainability, such as installing solar panels on the roof of the business or financing some piece of equipment or renovations to reduce the carbon footprint of the business. Or it might not be a loan for something like that initially but with the borrower having to show a genuine interest and the capacity to do so at some point in the near future.

"We didn't mean people had to be what we called 'dark green,'" Vince told me, "but they had to be on a journey. All of us are on a journey around sustainability, or for that matter equity and racism. We just wanted people to be on the journey, and then we could as part of our relationship with the client help move them along."

One of those networks turned out to be the growing community of B Corps (short for Certified B Corporations, which are certified by the nonprofit B Lab to meet an extensive set of standards for "social and environmental performance, accountability, and transparency"). Back in 2010, New Resource became one of the first banks in the United States to become a B Corp. To gain or maintain certification, companies must score at least 80 points out of a maximum of 200 on the B Corp assessment, which B Corps must conduct every three years. In some ways, it's analogous to a company getting a rating on its financial health from Standard and Poor's, Moody's, Fitch, or other investment rating agencies. Paying a living wage, increasing racial or gender representation among management or executive positions, or reducing a company's carbon footprint are just some of the ways companies can score points on the B Corp assessment. There are also questions for specific industries. Banks, for example, can get points for having loan products accessible to people without a social security number or having loan products serving as an alternative to payday loans. B Lab periodically updates or expands its assessment methodology, in consultation with global human rights experts, labor experts, environmental experts, and others. Since the first B Corps were certified in 2007, the number of B Corps has grown to nearly eight thousand around the world, including eighteen hundred in the United States. Only a few B Corps are banks, however. By 2024, there were just sixteen B Corp banks in the United States, including City First Bank and Southern Bancorp.

Organic foods would become one of New Resource Bank's major lines of business. A woman-led company founded in 1974, Veritable Vegetable is an organic produce distribution company, buying and picking up produce wholesale from organic farmers and delivering it safely to retail partners across California and a few other states. Vince found out that the organic food distribution firm was New Resource Bank's first depositor. A 2007 loan from New Resource allowed Veritable Vegetable to expand production while conserving energy through state-of-the-art cooler systems, heavy-duty doors, and specialized lighting, and a 2008 loan funded solar panels that still supplied 70 percent of its energy as of 2014.[4] In 2016, the bank financed the acquisition of the distributor's a second warehouse, across the street from its first. Later the bank financed the distributor's conversion to a fleet of hybrid trucks. "We're a customer of New Resource because we know New Resource is specializing in companies that are environmentally committed," Bu Nygrens, an owner of Veritable Vegetable, told the *New York Times* back in 2008. "We feel like for the first time in our 34-year history, we actually have a personal relationship with the people we're banking with."[5]

Companies like these were, in their own way, an underserved community, with industry convenings and networks where people gathered and sometimes lamented that there weren't any bankers out there who seemed to want to understand what they were doing. "We did a lot of deep dives.... Who are these people? What do they need? Where do they hang out? Why would they want a bank? How would they find us, and where could we find them?" Vince told me.

Getting to know an industry such as organic foods—who the players are, what the bottlenecks are, and just how things work—did more than just build or rebuild credibility for New Resource Bank. It also helped refine the bank's ability to understand and be prepared for the risks of lending to the sector. For organic food, that meant not just understanding who all the buyers and sellers are, but also establishing relationships up and down the entire supply chain—from farmer to processors to distributors to retailers and any brokers at any point along the chain. If the bank was taking a truckload of string beans as collateral, it needed to have a plan in place for what to do with those string beans if it ever needed to seize that collateral in case of a default. Even if the plan never gets set in motion, the bank needs to be able to tell its regulators that it has a plan and how the collateral they've got assigned to the loan would fetch a high enough price to minimize losses.

"When the regulators come through to do their exam, they're going to look through your portfolio and . . . pick out twenty or thirty companies they want to talk about," Vince told me. "But they always were satisfied with our responses. They learned along with us."

One Community under the Sun

One of the first larger solar deals Nina worked on at New Resource Bank involved five different B Corps, including her bank as well as Beneficial State Bank, based across the San Francisco Bay in Oakland. This deal provided solar installations at zero upfront costs for fifteen hundred homes in Arizona, California, Connecticut, Delaware, Maryland, Massachusetts, New Jersey, and New York. It combined tax credits as well as the use of power purchase agreements—contracts where a third-party investor "owns" the solar array in exchange for the tax credits, while the underlying homeowner agrees to purchase the power produced by the array at a rate lower than what they currently pay the local power company. As complicated as it is, this transaction setup is now a standard across the residential solar energy industry. The two banks serve as short-term lenders so that the installation companies can get to work while waiting for the tax credits and power purchase payments to start coming in after the arrays get turned on.

New Resource Bank found success at cultivating a sense of community among clients not necessarily tied to a specific place but rather to a specific set of values. In a way, that success ultimately led to the end of its run—although not to the end of the work it was doing.

Vince said he never thought that New Resource would sell off to another bank. In fact, some of his other early battles were with some of the bank's initial shareholders, who were very interested in selling the bank. Those investors were more of a Silicon Valley mindset. They said that they thought the bank was a really great idea, that it found "a great niche," and that they could build the bank and sell it to a bigger bank and get a big return on their original investment based on hype around its mission. Vince had to push back on them regularly.

"We did not want that kind of pressure," Vince told me. "I openly discussed with all our shareholders repeatedly, we're not for sale. We are mission maximizers, not profit maximizers. But there's always a financial component to [the] mission, because if you don't, if you aren't profitable, if you can't get a high enough return on equity, you're not going to be able to grow and be able to attract deposits."

A second group of investors, including RSF Social Finance and Triodos Bank, took a more long-term view. While they definitely didn't want to lose any money, they were more in it to see what kind of social and environmental impact the bank could have over a longer period of time. Like the orders of religious women who had deposited their savings into Shore Bank and some of the other banks and credit unions that later became known as Community Development Financial Institutions, these investors were looking for ways to invest their money that reflected their values, not just for highest financial returns.

In 2017, Vince announced his plans to retire the following year. That second batch of investors were among those who showered him with gratitude and praise. One surprising congratulatory call came in from another B Corp bank—Amalgamated Bank, in New York City.

Amalgamated Bank has its own unusual origin story. It was founded in 1923 by the leaders of the Amalgamated Clothing Workers of America, a garment workers union. In 2017, Amalgamated was significantly larger than New Resource, with around $4 billion in assets compared to $364 million for New Resource. It was also a very different kind of bank. Founded to serve union members, it had much more experience with individual depositors, and it has a huge portfolio of home mortgage loans as well as loans for rent-stabilized apartment buildings and co-ops. In more recent years, it has expanded its lending to nonprofits. Amalgamated did not do much of what New Resource did—lending to the organic foods sector or to solar and wind energy businesses and projects—nor did Amalgamated have much of a West Coast presence.

But it saw an opportunity to gain both a West Coast presence and significant expertise in green lending overnight by merging with New Resource Bank.

On the other side of the table, as New Resource Bank's reputation grew, the bank had been fielding an increasing number of loan requests from far beyond the Bay Area and California from clean energy companies, organic food companies, and other natural product companies that were having trouble finding lenders who understood their business models. In 2016, New Resource opened its first office outside San Francisco—in Boulder, Colorado. Although the call from Amalgamated to merge was unexpected, a merger started to make sense as a way to instantly add staff capacity as well as a much larger balance sheet to accommodate green lending requests from a much larger swath of the United States.

In other, deeper ways, Amalgamated and New Resource were similar. With a history and ownership embedded in the labor movement, Amalgamated famously had been the bank of choice to open an account for donations raised by the organizers of the original Occupy Wall Street encampment in New York's Financial District in 2011. In addition to being B Corps, New Resource Bank was and Amalgamated still is part of the Global Alliance for Banking on Values, a global network of financial institutions that believe in putting people and planet before profits. The alliance has its own assessment that prospective members must pass as a condition to join. Both banks believed in the broader idea that banking itself was never supposed to be just about making profits for shareholders.

"We were very slow and skeptical at first in evaluating [Amalgamated] and seeing if we thought there was a fit," Vince told me. "And we did think there was a fit, we did think that we provided them something that they didn't have, and they provided something for us that we didn't have."

New Resource and Amalgamated merged in 2018. Nina stayed with the newly merged institution and in 2019 was appointed western regional director for Amalgamated Bank. Her former boss at New Resource Bank, Bill Peterson, became Amalgamated's director of climate lending, with climate lending accounting for 36 percent of Amalgamated Bank's loan portfolio by 2022.[6] By the 2020s, solar panel installation loans had become an asset class, with hundreds and even thousands of loans being originated by specialized residential solar loan companies and sold to investors. As of June 2024, the Solar Energy Industries Association reported that there were more than 5 million solar energy systems installed across the United States, producing enough energy to power 36 million households.[7] That includes nearly 2 million residential and commercial solar installations in California alone.[8]

"There's been the evolution of us at the bank, taking that expertise but now with a larger balance sheet doing that at a larger scale, but at the same time there's been the evolution of the market," Nina told me. "Over time, a lot more banks have become more comfortable with solar lending. There's so much transaction history. Mainstream banks are doing it, the structure and terms and pricing [are] incredibly competitive. But there needs to be solar investment by banks on a large scale, and I think we're finally getting there."

A more recent and urgent challenge has been bringing more solar installations to low-income households, especially those who are renting their properties or live in mid- to large-scale apartment buildings. In Washington, DC, Amalgamated has been working with a local clean energy financing agency to facilitate deals for local solar array developers to install solar arrays in those settings.

Where Does Your Money Spend the Night?

When Vince first came to New Resource Bank, he knew that he needed to start building or rebuilding relationships with depositors who knew all too well the cold shoulders of a banking system that seemed at odds with their own personal values around people and planet. When speaking at environmental sustainability conferences or other activist or expert gatherings around the Bay Area, he asked attendees to think about something that's usually nothing more than an afterthought, even for those crowds: where they held their deposits. He would wave around a dollar bill as he delivered the question.

"I would say to people, 'Your money doesn't sleep at night. You sleep at night,'" he told me, "but your money is spending the night doing something somewhere. If you looked at a dollar bill as a magic carpet and you could get on that bill and ride around the world to see what your money is doing, would you be proud?'"

Over the next decade, the phrase made its way around the world and back again, among students and activists pushing university endowments to divest from fossil fuels. It made its way into Occupy Wall Street discussions in the wake of the financial crisis. And it made its way among so-called impact investors—people and institutions looking to invest in ways that directly addressed social or environmental challenges in addition to making a financial return.

"We considered copyrighting it, but part of being in the socially conscious world or equity conscious world is [that] you don't grab and hold, you give away," Vince told me. "It was the same with our business strategy. I shared our strategy all the time. I did not make a secret of it. The reason was, we wanted other people to do this. We wanted to be successful and tell other people how to do it."

Chapter 4

New Community Banks and Credit Unions in Communities of Color

The ancestors came calling for Daniel Johnson. He's the CEO of the new Arise Community Credit Union, which received its charter on March 18, 2024, making it Minnesota's first Black-led credit union and the state's first new credit union of any kind in more than a decade.

Daniel was about twelve years old when he moved from East St. Louis, his birthplace and home to one grandfather, to North Minneapolis, home to his other grandfather. He took after both of his grandfathers, who were entrepreneurs who started young. He cut grass, shoveled sidewalks, and had all kinds of side hustles as a kid. For him, North Minneapolis was a land of "milk and honey." But as Daniel grew, personally and professionally, the more it seemed his beloved North Minneapolis was falling into disinvestment. His first real job was at the McDonald's that used to be at Penn and Plymouth Avenues. His next job was down the street at King Supermarket. After taking an apprenticeship at a funeral home, he even dreamed of becoming a mortician. Then came retail jobs at a prominent downtown department store and eventually at a bank in North Minneapolis—a branch of one of the big four banks.

"I opened up half of North Minneapolis' checking accounts and teenage accounts for the people who are adults now," Daniel told me. Then, one of his former banking clients came to Daniel in 2021 and suggested that he throw his hat into the ring for CEO at the prospective Arise Community Credit Union. Daniel wasn't sure at first. He'd been moving up and was doing well financially and professionally selling insurance. He called his mother, a trailblazing Black woman who spent thirty years as an executive at AT&T, for advice. He asked her if she was proud of him, which she was, and to that he replied that maybe he'd stick it out on his current path.

"There was crickets on the line," Daniel told me. "I'm like, 'Mom, are you still there?' She said, 'Well, you know, your grandfather sold ice and coal on the back of a horse-driven buggy, and your other grandfather moved furniture for people in the hopes that one day that one of their descendants may go through the process and become a CEO of a financial institution. But no pressure.'"

As soon as he hung up the phone, Daniel sent in his resume. After a year-long selection process, Arise Community Credit Union's organizers named him as CEO-designate in October 2022 and submitted their application jointly to state and federal credit union regulators.

"This is what the community asked for after George Floyd's killing, after Philando Castile's killing and so many others," Daniel told me. "The community said, 'We don't want another park. We don't want another place just to throw flowers. We want something more tangible, something that we can have as an institution that will be around long after we're gone.'"

The Organizers

One week after a police officer on a routine traffic stop just north of Minneapolis shot and killed Philando Castile, a thirty-two-year-old African American man, more than community members from predominantly Black North Minneapolis gathered for a meeting to discuss systemic responses to the continued violence they were suffering at the hands of others. One theme that came up was investing in one another and divesting from systems and institutions that supported or enabled the kind of policing that routinely took the lives of their family, friends, and neighbors. They put pieces of butcher paper up on the walls around the room and filled them with ideas of what to do. At the end of the evening, they voted on which ideas to prioritize. The number one idea, receiving more than twice as many votes as any other, was to establish a Black-led financial institution in North Minneapolis.[1]

Chartering a new credit union today is like traversing a long-lost trail through the woods, one that used to be well-traveled but is now overgrown and littered with fallen trees and other obstacles that no one has had to navigate in many years. Prior to 1970, the federal government chartered five hundred to six hundred new credit unions across the country every year.[2] After plummeting to just a few dozen a year by the end of the 1980s, the numbers continued dwindling steadily.[3] From 2012 to 2022, the federal government chartered fewer than thirty new credit unions across the United States.[4]

They started with organizing. A group of those North Minneapolis community members and their allies formed a nonprofit, the Association for Black Economic Power, to lead the work of organizing a new Black-led credit union. Led at the time by community organizer Me'Lea Connelly, originally from the Bay Area, they started knocking on doors and canvassing at bus stops and shopping center parking lots, collecting data on potential members and recruiting as many as they could to sign letters pledging to deposit funds into the credit union when it opened. By the end of 2017, they'd collected more than eleven hundred pledges offering to deposit $3 million into a potential new credit union in North Minneapolis. With those pledges in hand, they went into a 2018 meeting with Minneapolis Mayor Jacob Frey with a bold ask: $500,000 a year for five years in city funding. The mayor said yes, at least to one year for $500,000. Later, as part of his first state of the city address, he even pulled out his own personal checkbook to write a check for a pledged deposit into the prospective credit union, at the time known as Village Financial Cooperative Credit Union.

The new credit union was on track to open its doors sometime in 2019 when a dispute broke out between board members and leadership of the Association for Black Economic Power. Accusations of misman-agement and defamation were hurled, and eventually there were lawsuits that are still unresolved. As for the prospective credit union, the saga derailed the chartering process. By 2020, when the nonprofit brought on new ex-ecutive director Debra Hurston, it basically needed to start over from scratch. A poll of its constituents generated a new name, Arise Community Credit Union. The community's interest in having its own financial institution in North Minneapolis only grew after the historic 2020 racial uprisings sparked by Minneapolis police officers' murder of Floyd, another African American, in a South Minneapolis neighborhood.

If having easier access to credit and other financial services than was traditionally offered was the only goal in North Minneapolis, it would have been easier, and much quicker, if the Association for Black Economic Power had created some kind of partnership with an existing financial institution to bring its loans and services to North Minneapolis. It would even have the power of the law on its side. Under the Community Reinvestment Act of 1977, which applies to banks but not credit unions, "regulated financial institutions have continuing and affirmative obligation to help meet the credit needs of the local communities in which they are chartered," including low-to-moderate income communities, but consistent with "safe and sound operations of such institutions."[5] It was a hugely controversial law when it was passed. Many who fought for it viewed it as one of the last pieces of civil rights era legislation. It was meant to discourage banks from redlining, which continued as a matter of practice even after it was technically outlawed in 1968. But the Community Reinvestment Act was watered down from the start. It says nothing explicitly about race or national origin, even though redlining is all about race and national origin. Instead, it directs federal banking regulators to evaluate each bank's lending in low- to moderate-income neighborhoods and to take those evaluations into account when considering approvals for changes such as opening or closing new branches, moving branches or headquarters, or for approving mergers with or acquisitions of other banks.

Even in its watered-down form, banking industry lobbyists vehemently opposed it. Only two banks testified to Congress in favor of the law: ShoreBank, and the country's oldest mutual bank at the time, the Philadelphia Savings Fund Society.[6] The passage of the Community Reinvestment Act was a tremendous victory for the community organizers who originated the idea for it, many of whom came from the Chicago area and had been fighting against redlining for years. After the act's passage, ShoreBank worked with community organizers in Chicago to share knowledge about banks' lending practices, sharpening their criticisms of banks. Many of the same organizers had successfully pushed for the Home Mortgage Disclosure Act of 1975, or HMDA (pronounced hum-dah), which required home mortgage lenders to collect, report, and disclose information to the public about their mortgage lending activity—including information on borrower race and ethnicity. Combined with the Community Reinvestment Act, HMDA data became crucial for organizers to hold banks accountable for redlining.

Organizers back then could make their case very plainly. If a bank held a certain amount in deposits in a certain county or set of zip codes, it should have a similar amount in loans to that same area. In 1977, when the Community Reinvestment Act was passed, banking was still very much local. As of 1976, 50 percent of bank branches still belonged to a bank headquartered in the same county as the branch location.[7] The law provided a platform for each community to hold mostly locally owned and locally controlled banks accountable. But as banks have grown larger and larger, it's become increasingly complex and challenging to enforce the Community Reinvestment Act. Regulators examine banks typically every three to five years, depending on the size of the bank and how well it performed since its last exam. Since at least 2006, 98 percent of banks have gotten a passing grade on their Community Reinvestment Act examinations.[8] Yet clear disparities still exist in access to credit based on race, ethnicity, gender, or national origin. On one recent Community Reinvestment Act exam, covering lending activity during the years 2019 to 2021, the twenty-third largest bank in the United States got the highest possible grade even though an analysis of 2021 HMDA data by bank watchdog groups clearly showed that the bank was almost completely avoiding making home mortgages in predominantly Black neighborhoods in several of its key markets, including Philadelphia, Buffalo, Hartford, Seattle, and even the bank's own hometown of Cleveland.

Despite the Community Reinvestment Act's shortcomings, grassroots groups like the Association for Black Economic Power can still leverage it as a way to create new partnerships and programs with larger financial institutions. But in the association's case, its members wanted more than that. Any time Debra brought up any such offers for a partnership, they were promptly turned away. The community still wanted a financial institution of its own.

"The mistrust in the banking community—it's not a small thing, and it can't be fixed overnight," Debra told me. "We're starting from the wrong spot if I have to protest in front of you to make you treat me right. Something's not right about that. So no one from our communities has ever asked me if we should just partner with a larger bank."

Seeking partners to help her create a new credit union, Debra reached out to trade associations—the Minnesota Credit Union Network and the African American Credit Union Coalition. Through these groups, the Association for Black Economic Power got connected to pro bono advisors to assist with everything from drafting their joint application for a state credit union charter and federal deposit insurance to choosing a "core processor"—that's the back-end technology for the credit union to process deposits, withdrawals, transfers, loans, and other transactions. The larger networks also helped with the CEO recruitment and selection process. The Minnesota Credit Union Network even took an unprecedented step to launch a capital campaign—the first campaign of its kind the network ever launched—for Arise Community Credit Union, raising $1 million in donations from nine of its members, covering most of Arise's required startup capital. On top of that, the capital campaign raised $4 million in deposits pledged from twenty of its members to be placed in new accounts at Arise after it opened for business. Those deposits from credit unions around the state will combine with $2 million and counting in deposit pledges for Arise coming from individuals or businesses in the Twin Cities. That will allow the credit union to start out with $6 million in assets, projecting to break even and have around $10 million in assets by its third year.

The Opportunity

Conditions for a new nonpredatory lender in Minnesota are better today than they have been in a very long time. New restrictions on payday lenders (offering short-term, high-interest, unsecured loans) could potentially be clearing out much of Arise's existing competition. After years of advocacy,[9] Minnesota Governor Tim Walz signed a bill in 2023 establishing an interest rate cap on loans in the state. Although advocates had been calling for a 36 percent rate cap, the final bill as signed into law set an overall cap of 50 percent while instituting a new requirement for lenders to evaluate a borrower's ability to repay for loans between 36 and 50 percent.

As of 2023, eighteen states plus the District of Columbia had established lending rate caps of 36 percent or below, according to the Center for Responsible Lending.[10] The caps have proven their effectiveness. Nebraska voters passed a 2020 ballot measure to establish a 36 percent rate cap in that state, and since then, payday lenders have disappeared across Nebraska, the *Omaha World-Herald* reported in May 2023.[11] In Arkansas, where the last payday loan storefront closed in 2009, retail borrowers say that they're better off and have been finding their way to safer, nonpredatory options.[12]

Arise's predatory competitors have definitely established that there is a market need that a new credit union can help meet. In 2021, thirty-nine licensed payday lending entities in Minnesota made 176,241 payday loans to 20,004 Minnesotans, according to the Minnesota Department of Commerce.[13] The average payday loan client in Minnesota took out nine payday loans in 2021, at an average loan amount of $365, and was charged an average of 197 percent interest per loan.[14] And there's a growing pile of evidence that payday lenders tend to place their storefronts in Black neighborhoods,[15] like those on the north side of Minneapolis. As those lenders retreat, Arise can be there to start picking up the pieces. And as that happens, it will be easier to start and scale up a small-dollar loan program than it ever was. For example, although it's still a source of some sticker shock for lenders, the back-end technology for banks or credit unions to process and manage a small-dollar consumer lending operation is becoming more reliable, efficient, and accessible. As a result, credit unions nationwide issued $227 million in payday alternative loans in 2022, topping the previous record of $174 million (set in 2019), according to a Pew analysis of data submitted to the National Credit Union Administration (NCUA).[16]

The Barber

Whenever Arlo Washington was short on cash as a youth in Little Rock, Arkansas, his barber, Royale, would let him get a haircut in exchange for sweeping the floors of the barbershop. Royale was a pillar of the community and impressed Arlo with how well he did for himself while creating opportunities for others as barbers in the shop. Little did Arlo know that picking up that broom to sweep his barber's floors in exchange for a haircut he couldn't afford would lead him to charter the first new credit union in Arkansas since 1996: People Trust Community Federal Credit Union, charter number 24940, approval date September 16, 2022.

Arlo's mother, a single-parent social worker, inspired him by the way she cared for her community. In 1995, two weeks before Arlo's high school graduation, she died of cancer. Pursuing his wildest dreams, he moved to New York City, where he briefly worked as a fashion model and a barber, but times were rough. He spent some nights sleeping in the back of the barbershop or just walking around all night until the sun came up, thinking about how to support his two younger sisters back home. After two years, he went back to Little Rock and enrolled in college. He managed to use some of the cash from his student loans to open his first barbershop. He figured, he told me, that if the loans were supposed to help him stay in school, one of the best ways for him to use the cash was to invest it in a source of income to pay for it. But that was in the early 2000s, when setting up a business didn't cost as much as it does today. Back then, Arlo only needed around $5,000 to start a barbershop in Little Rock. Arlo's reputation as a barber grew quickly. One barbershop became two, then three, and eventually seven barbershops. Arlo was spending so much time training new barbers for his barbershops that he eventually established his own barber college.

Meanwhile, in 2009, the last payday lending storefront in Arkansas closed for business after a statewide interest rate cap went into effect. A lot of folks in his community started coming to one of the few places where they knew someone they trusted to help them out with a little bit of cash in a pinch—their barber. It didn't take long for those kinds of requests to overwhelm Arlo's personal pockets. There were even community members coming to the barber college and asking for emergency loans—some because they'd previously gotten direct student loans from the barber college and some just because there was a sign on the side of the building that said, in all caps, "FINANCIAL AID IS AVAILABLE TO THOSE WHO QUALIFY." Arlo told me that he naturally had questions for those coming to him. "I said to them, 'Who's your banker?

What's your bank doing? Why your barber school? Why are you coming to us for loans?' And they said, 'There's nowhere else for us to get loans. My bank won't make me this loan.'"

Feeling obligated to serve the community, especially those who'd already graduated from the barber college, Arlo started having the barber college set aside up to $1,000 every month to make low-interest, small-dollar loans to the community. The loans went up to $250, with a six-month term and 5 percent interest. Things went on this way for a few years or so, all funded by the barber college. Arlo had talks with local banks and philanthropic foundations around Arkansas about contributing to the work, but nobody was interested in scaling up what the barber college was doing. As far as Arlo could tell, what the barber college was doing was too small or just invisible. It was below others' radar screens.

Around 2014, an uncle of Arlo's was visiting from Chicago, where he was a security guard at a CDFI. After seeing what Arlo was doing, his uncle told him about the CDFI Fund and that what the barber college was doing with its small-dollar loans definitely fell within the realm of CDFI work. His uncle suggested that Arlo should look into getting CDFI certification. Upon looking into the extensive application for CDFI certification, Arlo concluded that it wasn't worth the effort. But two years later, with demand for loans rising more and more each year, it was, and in 2016, People Trust Community Loan Fund got its CDFI certification as a nonbank, nonprofit, community development loan fund.

Two years later, Arlo was on the verge of shutting down and dissolving the loan fund. Certification hadn't proved fruitful up to that point. Despite applying for funding, the loan fund still hadn't gotten any support from the CDFI Fund, nor any other support from banks or philanthropy or local government. Operating out of a shipping container converted into an office in the parking lot next to the barber college, the loan fund was starting to become a drain on the college's cash reserves. Then one day in 2018, as Arlo was walking across the parking lot from the barber college to the shipping container and preparing to tell the loan fund's one employee that it was time to shut it all down, his phone rang. It was a call from another colleague letting Arlo know that after two years of nothing, People Trust Community Loan Fund had finally gotten an award from the CDFI Fund. After news of that grant got out, the Winthrop Rockefeller Foundation suddenly ponied up a $90,000 grant for the loan fund. Arlo promptly spent that on building out the loan fund's online lending platform, an urgent need as online lenders were increasingly coming into the Little Rock market with fast, user-friendly—yet predatory—loan products.

Arlo might have stopped at the loan fund. But since finally cracking the CDFI certification nut and getting some early grants, he had also learned about the Community Reinvestment Act and how banks can meet some of their obligations under the law by making either loans or grants to nonbank CDFIs like People Trust Community Loan Fund. He started asking different banks in the region, particularly when a merger was announced—like when Memphis-based First Horizon Bank and Louisiana-based Iberia Bank announced their merger in 2019—if they were interested in supporting his CDFI through such an arrangement. Under the Community Reinvestment Act, mergers or acquisition announcements are moments for community-based groups to stand up and express their concerns that one or both banks isn't meeting their needs and therefore the merger should be denied. Like countless other community groups before them, People Trust sent a comment letter to regulators during the First Horizon–Iberia merger approval period detailing its concerns that the banks weren't meeting the needs of low-income communities. That eventually sparked conversations Arlo had with First Horizon, which eventually led to a $100,000 donation from First Horizon to People Trust. Soon other banks and more foundations started writing checks to support the loan fund.

The COVID-19 pandemic sparked the idea to go one step further as a financial institution, as well as providing People Trust with a windfall of cash to do it. One part of the federal government's response to the pandemic was the $800 billion Paycheck Protection Program. The goal of the program was to provide financial assistance in the form of forgivable loans to small businesses in exchange for keeping their employees on payroll instead of laying them off as the United States—and the world—shut down to contain the spread of the virus. Businesses would get the loans and use them to cover payroll and other eligible expenses; a few months later, they could submit paperwork proving that they spent the money on eligible expenses and get the entire loan amount, including interest, forgiven. Although the US government has other programs in which it makes loans directly to small businesses in times of crisis, the Paycheck Protection Program flowed through the Small Business Administration's existing network of private lenders who were part of the agency's loan guarantee programs. The idea was that the lenders who already have relationships with small businesses would provide the quickest possible avenue to roll out the program and evaluate applications to minimize fraud. There still ended up being a lot of fraud in the program, however. Also, by relying on the Small Business Administration's existing network of private lenders—almost entirely banks or credit unions, the vast majority of which are owned by and primarily serve White communities—the Paycheck Protection Program suffered from the existing racial and gender disparities in access to those lenders. In the year prior to the pandemic,[17] the Small Business Administration's main loan guarantee program made just 26.5 percent of its loans to businesses owned by people of color (12.1 percent Asian, 9.1 percent Hispanic, 4.5 percent African American, and 0.8 percent American Indian). Just 18 percent went to majority-women-owned businesses.

The Paycheck Protection Program's early rounds failed to reach the most vulnerable small businesses—those at the lower end of the revenue scale, whose owners are disproportionately people of color. Even if they had business checking accounts at mainstream banks, Black and Hispanic business owners are less likely to have a lending relationship with their bank, which was the key factor in who got first and easiest access to the Paycheck Protection Program. Arlo heard all kinds of frustration with big banks from clients of People Trust, not to mention all the barbershop owners who'd previously graduated from his barber college. On more than one occasion, a frustrated client with a business of their own asked if they could move their bank accounts to People Trust, but up to that point, the CDFI was still just a non-depository institution.

As the pandemic dragged on, Congress made changes to the Paycheck Protection Program that were intended to ensure better access for historically marginalized communities. Subsequent rounds of funding within the program contained set-asides and rules changes that allowed more nonbank CDFIs to become lenders within the program, including

People Trust. But the frustrations with banks continued. After People Trust approved Paycheck Protection Program loans in the Small Business Administration's system, some banks initially refused to accept the wire transfers from People Trust, fearing that they were fraudulent transactions. In other cases, banks accepted the wire transfers but then immediately froze those accounts, also for fear of fraud. Few at big banks knew who People Trust was, so those transactions seemed to raise red flags. In other cases, banks ghosted clients after taking all their information, and People Trust then had to go into the Small Business Administration's application platform for lenders to see what happened and make sure they weren't about to submit a duplicate application for the same client. Some clients had to go back to the banks that ghosted them to withdraw applications that were stalled in the system for whatever reason just so that People Trust could submit a new application on their behalf. But the most vulnerable businesses Arlo saw were those that didn't even have a bank account because their owners either didn't trust banks or the banks took their credit history as a red flag to avoid doing business with them.

The Paycheck Protection Program stopped taking new applications for good at the end of May 2021. By that point, People Trust had successfully made around $50 million in Paycheck Protection Program loans to around twenty-six hundred businesses nationwide—its numbers boosted by its timely entrée into online lending back in 2019 combined with the national frustration with big banks that sent so many frustrated small business owners scouring the internet for other options. As part of the Paycheck Protection Program, the Small Business Administration paid fees to lenders for administering the loans and loan forgiveness procedures—5 percent of the loan value for loans up $350,000; 3 percent for loans of more than $350,000 and less than $2,000,000; and 1 percent for loans above $2,000,000.[18] People Trust ended up earning about $4.2 million in fees from the Paycheck Protection Program. It was a windfall for the loan fund, which put $3 million of it back out on the street in new loans.

Amid all those frustrations with banks, with clients asking if they could move their money to People Trust, and seeing a bit more of how the process worked from the inside, Arlo started batting around the idea of People Trust creating its own depository institution. He talked about it with clients, board members, staff, and even the security guard at the shipping container where People Trust was still operating in the fall of 2021. Arlo stayed two hours late one evening to type a long email to the NCUA, expressing the interest and need for a new credit union focused on low-income and Black communities in Little Rock. Much to his surprise, he got a reply back saying that it looked as if there was a strong basis for a new credit union in Little Rock, and encouraging him to go ahead with the full charter application.

Federal credit union regulators do have a history of occasionally encouraging development of new credit unions, particularly in low- to moderate-income communities. The Bureau of Federal Credit Unions, which regulated credit unions from 1934 to 1970, launched Project Moneywise in 1966 as part of the Lyndon Johnson administration's War on Poverty.[19] The program provided grants and a four-week training course in credit union management.[20] By the time the program ended in 1972, the federal government had chartered 3,667 new credit unions, making up 28 percent of all 13,133 federally chartered credit unions.[21] But that interest has waxed and waned since the NCUA was created in 1970.

In 2017, the NCUA created the Office of Credit Union Resources and Expansion, or CURE Office, combining some earlier functions with new resources and a new commitment to streamlining the credit union chartering process. In some ways, it mimics how the Federal Aviation Administration provides resources for the airline industry to recruit and train new pilots or how the US Department of Agriculture has extension programs and university partnerships to promote and support the agriculture sector. It was the CURE Office that replied to Arlo's initial contact and worked closely with him and the People Trust Community Loan Fund to get through the charter application process, which took about a year. Even with more help from the NCUA, parts of the process are tedious and time consuming. The most challenging part for Arlo was selecting board members. He needed to find board members who had strong ties to the community—people whom he and the community could trust with setting policies like interest rates or fee structures but who would also pass NCUA muster on background checks and credit checks. And, unlike bank board directors who typically earn a stipend, credit union board memberships are unpaid, volunteer positions. Some of People Trust's initial picks were rejected because of their personal credit history.

By contrast, the marketing plan on the charter application was relatively easy for Arlo, somebody with decades of experience as a small business owner in the Little Rock community, first as a barber and later as a barber college operator. He knows the local drive-time talk radio shows and can pick out the best spots for billboards. Word of mouth has been surprisingly strong, even more so than Arlo expected after a few years of operating as a loan fund. Senior citizens in particular have been excited to have a chance to move their money to a homegrown financial institution right in their backyard.

Operating People Trust Community Loan Fund for several years prior to the application turned out to be a big help. As part of the chartering process, credit union organizers need to survey a large enough sample size of their intended community about credit needs that other institutions aren't meeting: what kinds of accounts, what kinds of loans do members of the target community need and want that they can't get anywhere else, and so on. It was easy enough to send the survey link to the thousands of people on the loan fund's existing email contact list and social media until there were enough replies. The loan fund and its lending track record also strengthened People Trust's credit union charter application.

The plan is for the credit union to take over the small-dollar consumer loans that the loan fund has been doing all these years, including payday loan alternatives and car loans. The loan fund staff have experience making those loans successfully under the nonprofit, which they could point to as part of the application for a credit union charter. With the credit union in place, the loan fund can move into making larger loans for small business growth and economic development projects perceived as too risky for the credit union—kind of like ShoreBank or City First or any of the other CDFIs that operate as a hybrid of a nonprofit and a depository institution. And with the nonprofit loan fund serving as the "sponsor" of the credit union—the role usually played by a church or employer or some other membership organization—the loan fund can use part of the remaining windfall from the Paycheck Protection Program to subsidize the credit union in its startup phase.

People Trust also used a piece of the Paycheck Protection Program windfall to buy a former bank branch to use for the credit union. It turned out that the previous landlord had also sold everything inside the branch, from furniture to equipment and even the bank vault, so the loan fund had to buy all that anew.

All the work was worth it to embed the sense of self-determination that comes from being able to control at least some of the flow of money at the community level. "We wanted to control the flow of capital and where it went and who it went to because we hadn't had control for a long time and been able to do anything about the issues that our communities face outside of getting together and talking about it," Arlo told me. "At the end of the day, you still gotta go to the bank to settle your transaction. When [financial assistance] comes through from the government, it goes to a bank that doesn't even think twice about your neighborhood and what you need—they're only going to their big customers. So we got tired of that. And we wanted to be able to make a difference, you know, a real difference, and bring about some transformational change for generations to come. So that's why we did it."

People Trust Community Federal Credit Union is rebuilding that sense of control, one account at a time. As of December 2023, the credit union had more than four hundred members and more than $4 million in assets.

The Homecoming

Kevin Boyce had never thought about starting up his own bank. He's a trailblazer to be sure, as an African American from Columbus, Ohio, who previously held a managing director position at a Black-owned firm in the White-dominated world of investment banking. He also served eight years on the Columbus City Council, served two years as state treasurer of Ohio—the first African American member of the Democratic Party to hold a statewide office in Ohio—and spent four years in the Ohio State Assembly. In 2016, Kevin became the first African American elected as a Franklin County commissioner, the county that includes Columbus. In May 2020, he was participating in a Black Lives Matter demonstration in downtown Columbus when a melee broke out.

Police officers pepper sprayed the crowd, including Kevin and several other elected officials. Later that night, Kevin told me, he was talking on the phone with a good friend, emergency room surgeon Kamran Haydar, and reflecting on the progress that has and hasn't occurred since the end of slavery, the end of legal segregation, and the civil rights movement. The racial disparity in wealth stuck out as one area where there has been basically zero progress over all this time. After hanging up the phone, for the first time in his life Kevin went online and searched how to start a bank. At that moment, there were no other Black-owned or Black-led banks in Ohio, and there hadn't been a newly chartered Black-owned or Black-led bank anywhere in the United States for nearly twenty years.

Kevin would need to raise a lot more than the $43,000 adjusted for inflation that Maggie Walker raised in startup capital for her bank, Richmond's St. Luke Penny Savings Bank, back in 1903. On top of that, although Maggie had spent time observing how White-owned banks operated as part of her preparation to charter and run her own bank, she had zero experience running a bank. Today, it's just about impossible to obtain a bank charter without having a significant amount of banking experience among the proposed founding board members or management team. Regulators view prior experience as essential to safe and sound operations for a bank. Fortunately for Kevin, his friend Jordan Miller had just retired from a high-level management position after a forty-year career at a large regional bank. Jordan came out of retirement to serve as Adelphi's founding CEO, joining Kevin and Kamran as co-founders of Adelphi Bank.

The founders considered other options as vehicles to invest in Black communities in and around Columbus, options that may have required less startup capital and less red tape than starting a bank and options that Maggie Lena Walker didn't necessarily have in her time. Adelphi Bank's cofounders could have started a fintech, a startup company promising some way of providing smartphone-based or online banking options that would use some kind of sophisticated algorithm to make loans to Black people or Black businesses. With his business connections from investment banking and public finance, Kevin could have easily found a few angel investors to seed something like that, especially amid the fervor around racial justice tied to the 2020 police killings of Floyd, Breonna Taylor, and other unarmed Black people.

They also looked into starting a credit union. One of the immediate needs they saw, however, was the need to invest in local Black businesses to help them grow and create more net worth for their owners as well as create more jobs for Black workers. Although it hasn't always been this way, credit union regulators currently only allow newly chartered credit unions to make personal loans or car loans during their first few years. Adelphi hopes to meet those needs in some way, but it couldn't be limited to that condition initially.

They could have started a nonbank CDFI loan fund, especially since an increasing number of private foundations and private investors are becoming more and more accustomed to working with CDFI-certified loan funds or even other loan funds that aren't CDFI certified but have some intentional mission around racial justice or community development. A loan fund can be very useful, especially because regulators aren't combing through its loan records on a regular basis looking for what they think might be risky loans. But they can also be limited by what their funders are willing to support at any given moment. Sometimes major funders also end up with board seats, which can influence loan fund lending standards that start to look more and more like what major funders are familiar with versus what communities might need. In terms of potential funding sources, philanthropic sources are just a drop in the ocean compared with deposits.

After reviewing all the options, Adelphi's cofounders still believed that a fully chartered commercial bank was the best starting point and that it could serve as a kind of hub or platform that could branch out later to do some of those other things—like get CDFI certification for the bank, create an affiliated CDFI-certified loan fund, or even create its own affiliated fintech company. They believed that the Black-owned businesses or other businesses that Adelphi helps start and grow might also need or want a place to bank, so why not keep those deposits on Adelphi's own balance sheet where they'll support other investments in the community instead of sitting on a big bank balance sheet supporting investments somewhere else. The workers at those growing businesses might already have a bank, but according to one survey, Black workers are the most likely to be unbanked or underbanked,[22] so they're also more likely than other workers to be looking for a bank they can trust to hold their deposits. Having a Black-led bank to serve Black communities isn't the only change Kevin sees as necessary for racial justice in Columbus, but to him it is definitely one of the necessary changes. As Kevin told me, "The financial and the wealth gap issue has to be [part of] a mosaic or puzzle of things that we work to address. When you can factor in a better equation for homeownership, when you can factor in a better equation for entrepreneurship and capital access, when you can factor in a better equation for savings for college or other investments, then you can begin to change the narrative that our country has struggled for so long with." As for the future, he said, "We've got a ways to go, but if we begin to change each piece of the puzzle in a positive direction, then it becomes something that looks beautiful when it comes together like a mosaic often does."

All Adelphi Bank's nine founding board members—seven of whom are Black—invested some of their own personal wealth as startup capital for the bank, and they found a few other startup investors from Black communities in Columbus. But unlike every other Black bank before them, they went outside Black communities to raise the rest of the $24 million in startup capital for the bank. They started with a list of about 250 contacts drawn from their previous social and business networks—from Jordan's forty-year career in mainstream commercial banking to Kevin's career as a local elected official, former Ohio state treasurer, and investment banker. Some contacts had their own personal wealth to invest; some had access to institutional investment dollars that might otherwise be invested in stocks, bonds, real estate, or private equity; and some potentially had access to both. The minimum investment was $50,000, and the opportunity was restricted to institutions or people considered "accredited investors"—that's the US Securities and Exchange Commission's term for somebody with a net worth of at least $1 million or income of at least $200,000 for the previous two years.

Although Adelphi's founders wanted local investors to provide the seed capital for their bank, they didn't want small investors who could be at risk of losing all their life savings in a single investment. They made it clear to everyone that any startup investment is a high-risk investment, whether it's a startup bank or a startup social media platform. In the case of a startup bank, especially one that was promising to focus on working with Black businesses or Black developers, the potential rewards—despite the high risk—are hardly exorbitant, and it will take time to see any financial returns, they emphasized. Regulations don't allow the bank to pay dividends to shareholders for its first three years. Since it went public, Ponce Bank has continually communicated to its shareholders that it has zero plans or aspirations to ever pay dividends. Investing in a new community bank, especially one serving a historically marginalized community, isn't really for investors who are shopping around for the highest, quickest bang for their buck.

"Some people wanted us to have higher numbers, and I said to them, 'That's like buying a Cadillac and asking how much [miles per gallon] it gets,'" Jordan told me. "'If that's your question, you're probably not a good investor for us. That's not who we are, that's not what this is. You're either trusting that we can do this mission, or you don't—and if you don't, then don't invest.' And I told that to a lot of people."

Most people they talked to didn't invest. In the end, out of the hundreds of people they contacted over the course of about year, just twenty-five institutions and approximately fifty individuals ended up investing. With $24 million in shares scattered across seventy-five shareholders, most of whom are not Black, Adelphi Bank isn't technically a Black-owned bank. Instead, it is meeting the Federal Deposit Insurance Corporation's designation as a minority-depository institution based on the majority of its board and its target market being African American. Also, the shares sold to large institutional investors were nonvoting shares, so the founding board, which is majority-Black, retains control over the bank.

In a way, Adelphi's business plan is also a reflection of its ownership and leadership structure. Although the bank prioritizes serving disinvested Black communities, its business plan also leans on serving other underserved communities around Columbus in all the typical ways that community banks traditionally do: focusing on small businesses, commercial real estate, and first-time home mortgages for those who don't qualify under prevailing lending terms. Although Adelphi may come up with loan terms and services designed to make credit more widely available to Black borrowers, it doesn't have to make those more-inclusive loan terms exclusive to Black borrowers; it can make those same terms available to all borrowers in the bank's footprint, regardless of race. Reaching those other borrowers will be key for Adelphi's long-term sustainability because no community bank can really be successful if it limits itself to serving just 25 percent of its community—that's the percentage of Black residents in Franklin County, Ohio.[23]

Adelphi Bank's charter and deposit insurance approval came through on January 18, 2023. By the end of that year, it had opened more than five hundred accounts and had nearly $43 million in assets, including loans for new developers of color working on affordable housing and other real estate projects around the Columbus area and $6 million in commercial loans and lines of credit.

It's proved to be a kind of homecoming for Jordan. The new Adelphi Bank was named after Adelphi Building Savings and Loan, a Black-owned bank founded in 1921 to serve the historically segregated Black communities on the east side of Columbus. Jordan and the founders of the old Adelphi turned out to be fellow members of the same historically Black fraternity. Jordan grew up in the area and remembers it as a thriving commercial district anchored by the Lincoln Theatre, built by a Black developer in 1928 to serve Black patrons who were either forbidden entry to or relegated to the balcony sections of the Ohio capital city's downtown theaters. The theater was just a few blocks down the same street as the old Adelphi. It's unclear when the old Adelphi folded as the neighborhood fell victim to "urban renewal" in the form of Interstate 71 being constructed right through the area. The Lincoln Theatre barely survived the neighborhood's decline, closed in 1974, and gradually fell into disrepair before the city finally took over ownership, restoring and reopening it in 2009. The old Adelphi building became a funeral home for many years but had already been shuttered by the time it was demolished in 2019 to clear the way for a new mixed-use development. The new development did manage to incorporate the facade from the old Adelphi building exactly where it previously stood, just a few steps away from the new Adelphi Bank.

Chapter 5

New Banks and Credit Unions for the Environment

T erri Mickelsen and about nine thousand friends aren't waiting to jump into the green revolution. They're members of Clean Energy Credit Union, where Terri is CEO, and since 2017, they've invested more than $200 million in clean energy or other green loans for member households across the United States. These investments have offset an estimated 700,000 tons of carbon dioxide emissions annually—equivalent to taking 152,000 gas-powered vehicles off the road permanently. Every month, they make another $6 million to $8 million in green loans.

The roots of Clean Energy Credit Union date to 2013 when a group of solar energy companies was struggling to reach the next level of scale. Two years earlier, a bunch of them had already come together to form Amicus Solar Cooperative, which pools their collective buying power to negotiate more affordable prices from suppliers of modules, inverters, and all the rest of the components that go into building and installing solar arrays. But even with that mechanism in place, the up-front cost of installing solar arrays was too much for the average household, and the banking industry still hadn't figured out how it could structure a loan that would work for these situations. Blake Jones, cofounder of Namaste Solar in Colorado (which itself is a worker-owned cooperative), pitched the idea of launching a credit union to members of Amicus. Four other companies signed on (two in Arizona, one in Ohio, and one in Vermont) and began looking into the chartering process.

That founding group recruited Terri in 2016 to help them navigate the chartering process and get the credit union up and running. She came in with more than twenty-five years of experience in credit unions, starting off as a teller. Although early discussions with the regulators at the National Credit Union Administration were encouraging, the prospective credit union faced tough questioning from the agency about its planned business model as the process went on. With no established market for solar lending, regulators were nervous about granting a charter and deposit insurance coverage to a credit union with a business plan that seemed highly speculative. Eventually, to help diversify into offerings that were somewhat more familiar to regulators, the credit union added car loans for electric vehicles as well as loans for electric bicycles to its business plan.

Approximately three hundred credit unions across the United States already had some kind of green loan product available by 2023, according to Inclusiv, formerly known as the National Federation of Community Development Credit Unions.[1] Based in Puerto Rico, Cooperativa Jesus Obrero has financed six hundred solar panel installations across twenty-eight municipalities on the island since it started doing so in the aftermath of Hurricane Maria in 2017.[2] In a survey of just thirty credit unions, Inclusiv tallied up more than $1 billion in green loans. The loans went for everything from solar panels to electric vehicles, improved insulation, weatherproofing, air-source heat pumps, geothermal heat pumps, electric bicycles, and more. These mostly smaller institutions have already been taking the lead on smaller-scale transactions that are just as important for decarbonizing the economy as larger projects around energy production and distribution networks.

Indian Shores

When you check in at Legacy Vacation Resorts Indian Shores, located on a barrier island along the Gulf Coast of Florida, your room key has a number on it telling you how many trees were planted to offset the carbon produced by an average stay at the resort. The resort has been continually working to reduce the carbon offsets per stay—finding alternatives to plastics, like your room key, which is made out of bamboo, and supplying 80 percent of the resort's electricity through on-site rooftop solar power. It's enough solar power production that the resort's savings on its monthly energy bill exceed the monthly payments for the loan that Legacy Vacation Resorts took out to install the solar array.

CEO Jared Meyers spent about two years looking for someone willing to make that loan. Legacy Vacation Resorts is a B Corp, and Jared is a B Corp evangelist of sorts. He also runs a B Corp real estate company called Salt Palm Development. Jared has set a goal for Legacy Vacation Resorts to be on 100 percent renewable energy at all its locations—four in Florida, two in Colorado, one in Nevada, and one New Jersey—by 2030. But none of the lenders Jared contacted at first were willing to work with him on making it a reality, including some lenders that have had business relationships with him going back to 2009 when he founded Legacy Vacation Resorts. The other lenders were all scared away by the complexity of the underlying ownership structures for each location. When Jared acquired each of his company's resorts from their previous owners, his company inherited their multilayered ownership structures with a variety of time-share arrangements. Most of the resorts go back to the 1980s; one dates to 1956.

Jared eventually worked with a community bank to finance solar arrays at his company's four Florida resorts. Headquartered in St. Petersburg, Florida, Climate First Bank was chartered in June 2021 with a specific mission to tackle climate change. It's one of only a few depository institutions across the United States to have ever had such a mission since its inception. Climate First Bank is also a B Corp, and Jared is one of its founding board members. By the end of 2023, Climate First Bank had already grown to $540 million in assets, with $461 million in loans and $480 million in deposits. Not every loan Climate First makes is specifically for something related to climate or environmental sustainability, but in 2023, the bank financed $35 million in solar loans for businesses and $83 million in solar loans for households.[3]

Climate First Bank is the third community bank that founder Ken LaRoe has chartered over his career and the second to have a mission of green lending. The first time Ken chartered a bank was back in 1999. Born and raised in Central Florida, Ken had been working in the Florida banking industry since 1982 and had seen many other community banks chartered and eventually get acquired by larger banks. Bank mergers and acquisitions were so commonplace by the late 1990s that chartering and selling community banks had become a kind of money-making model for established community bank executives and their friends. You could charter a new bank, pick off customers who weren't happy with how their bigger banks were treating them, especially small business owners, build up a new bank's balance sheet, and after five or ten years sell the bank and make a healthy profit for your shareholders. In the late 1990s, Florida banking regulators only required a minimum initial shareholder investment of $5 million to charter a new bank. After raising the necessary startup capital from a few hundred people in his local network of banking and business contacts in central Florida, Ken chartered Florida Choice Bank in 1999. It grew to more than $400 million in assets by 2006, when he sold it to a regional bank based in Alabama. Two years later, that regional bank was acquired by Royal Bank of Canada, or RBC, Canada's largest bank and one of the top fifty largest banks in the world.

With his share of the proceeds from the sale of Florida Choice Bank, Ken set out to kick off his early retirement on an RV tour around the United States with his wife, Cindy, a physician. Ken and Cindy are both avid cyclists and nature lovers. Along the way, Ken started reading the book *Let My People Go Surfing* by the founder of Patagonia, the famous outdoor clothing and equipment company—which is also a B Corp.[4] Reading that book got Ken hooked on the idea that businesses couldn't be only about making a profit; rather, they could be about something bigger and more purposeful. It inspired him to help prove that point by returning to Florida and chartering another community bank, one that would have a specific mission to have a positive impact in terms of environmental sustainability. But this was still back around 2007, and solar and other renewable energy markets still weren't established enough for regulators to understand how they could be a viable component of a bank's business plan. Ken had to overcome a lot of resistance from regulators to include green lending even as just a small component of a bank's initial business plan. It had to be in the initial business plan because once the regulators grant a new bank charter, a new bank has to stick with its initial business plan during its de novo period—the technical jargon referring to a bank's first three years in business. To raise a bit more startup capital, Ken went back to some of the investors from his first bank, brought in others they knew might be interested, and in the end raised $17.2 million in startup capital for what became First Green Bank. This feat was all the more impressive as the capital raising took place during the height of the financial crisis. First Green got its charter approval and opened its doors in 2009. Like New Resource Bank in San Francisco, First Green became one of the leading early solar installation lenders and one of earliest banks in the United States to get certified as a B Corp. By 2018, when Ken sold it to another, much larger Florida-based bank, First Green had grown to $800 million in assets.

That sale ended up breaking Ken's heart. The larger bank had courted Ken on the idea that it would take First Green's early work around green lending and expand it to its much larger branch network across the region. Ken told me that he thought he could stick around as a green lending expert at the larger bank. But it became clear after acquisition that the bigger bank wasn't going to continue with the values-based mission and work that Ken had started at First Green Bank. So he left—and set out on another cross-country RV tour with Cindy. This trip was less celebratory, more soul searching. He said that he'd wake up each morning thinking to himself that he would get back to Florida and start another bank, and by the end of the day, he'd talk himself out of going through the stress and the headaches of pursuing that idea. Cindy eventually talked him into making the leap yet again—a third time—to start a new bank that would be even more deeply grounded in its environmental mission.

This time around, regulators were more than receptive of a proposed bank business plan that had an emphasis on green lending. They even showed up to help celebrate a ribbon cutting at Climate First Bank's first branch location in St. Petersburg. Ken ultimately raised $44 million in startup capital for Climate First—more than twice the $17 million he originally planned to raise. After only one year, the bank was growing so fast that it needed to go back to regulators to ask permission to raise a second round of startup capital in 2023, raising another $35 million just to keep up with its capital requirements.

Some of those dollars came from investors who had invested in Ken's first one or two community banks, and they simply trusted that he would make them money yet again. Some of those dollars came from the growing number of investors who are considering some kind of social or environmental impact in their investment decisions. These investors come in all shapes and sizes, from high-net-worth individuals and families to philanthropic foundations to pension funds, insurance companies, and investment funds managed by some of the largest investment companies in the world. They use different labels to signify various strategies, like environmental, social, and governance (ESG) investing, referring to the factors that an ESG investor might consider when deciding to invest or not invest. Environmental factors could include avoiding fossil fuel companies and seeking out clean energy companies as investments. Social factors could include everything from investing in companies that pay at least a living wage to all their employees to avoiding investments in prisons, guns, or the military industrial complex. Governance factors could mean looking for companies with strong internal policies around pay equity or being a worker-owned company. As of 2022, about $8.4 trillion in assets were managed using ESG investment strategies.[5]

There's been some blowback against these kinds of socially conscious investment strategies. Some of it has been political backlash against any use of nonfinancial factors to make investment decisions. States like Texas and even Climate First Bank's home state of Florida have passed measures targeting banks and investment management firms that use these strategies. It hasn't meaningfully affected Climate First Bank's business just yet. On the other hand, it could be a hidden blessing as Florida residents look for ways to fight back against elected officials with whom they might disagree. At the same time, however, some of these so-called socially responsible investments have turned out to be not as socially responsible as advertised or have been found to be a form of greenwashing, an attempt by some to launder their reputations or distract from the harm they might still be supporting. Getting certified as a B Corp is a way for some like Climate First to stand out if they're looking to raise startup capital or deposits from ESG investors.

Walden Local

In 2013, Charley Cummings and his wife started a sustainable food company in Concord, New Hampshire, called Walden Local. It's a direct-to-consumer business, purchasing grass-fed beef and pasture-raised pork and chicken from farmers in the region and delivering it right to consumers' doorsteps. Farmers, food processors, distributors, and consumers have all been excited to join them in helping build a more sustainable food system, but the banks didn't share that excitement. As Walden Local was growing its customer base, the businesses upstream in its supply chain were having trouble accessing the right type of capital to scale up alongside them. Although Charley's company was able to connect with private investors who believed in its mission and its model, his suppliers weren't necessarily looking to take on additional owners to invest in their farms or food processing facilities. They weren't a good fit for venture capital investors, the kind of investors who eventually need your company to grow large enough so they can cash out their shares after your company goes public; rather, they just needed working capital lines of credit to scale up and meet larger order sizes. But they couldn't find any banks willing to work with them. Unlike the rest of the United States, there just weren't bankers left around the Northeast who specialized in food and agriculture lending. Bankers didn't understand their businesses or the sustainable food sector well enough to do so.

The farm credit system, established by Congress in 1916, provides financing for farmers and the food industry, but like the broader banking system, farm credit entities have consolidated. There were once eight farm credit entities serving the Northeast, but by the time Charley launched his company, there was only one, and it had grown in size to the point where it was no longer interested in working with small- and midscale producers, manufacturers, distributors, consumer brands, and trade brands like Walden Local and its suppliers. Walden Local did what it could by prepaying for its orders, essentially lending money up front for suppliers to scale up production, but it wasn't long before the company was reaching its own limits with prepaying orders.

To fill in the gap, Charley landed on a very old solution: a mutual bank. In October 2022, Walden Mutual Bank opened for business, becoming the first new mutual bank to open its doors across the United States since 1973. By the end of 2023, Walden Mutual—specializing in local food and agriculture lending across New England and New York—had more than two thousand depositors, $55 million in deposits, and $61 million in assets, including loans to farmers, organic food production facilities, and distributors. It's even been looking into projects to build solar arrays over grazing areas to add some income for farmers.

Charley chose the mutual bank structure for a few reasons, starting with the bank's intention to be around for a long time. The mutual bank model has proven its longevity. Of the 426 remaining mutual banks across the United States, more than half were established prior to the start of the Great Depression in 1929, including at least a hundred mutual banks established before 1900 that are still in business today.[6]

Another reason the mutual bank model appealed to Charley was the prevalence of cooperatives in the agriculture space. Grocery store shelves everywhere are lined with products from farmer-owned cooperatives like Ocean Spray, Land-O-Lakes, and Organic Valley. The remaining farm credit entities are also technically producer-owned cooperative financial institutions. Rural electric cooperatives have a long history of delivering power to farmers and rural towns across the United States. Farmers and food entrepreneurs have a history of trust and doing business with cooperatives. Charley first looked into starting a credit union, a much more common example of a cooperatively owned and governed financial institution, but there were a few reasons it wasn't the best fit. Regulators today, for example, don't allow new credit unions to do commercial lending in their first two or three years. Beyond that, current laws limit credit union business lending to 12.25 percent of a credit union's assets—unless a majority of the members come from low-income census tracts. These restrictions just didn't make sense for a new financial institution whose primary clients were going to be agriculture and food businesses. But a mutual bank ownership structure is similar to a credit union in that it is ultimately accountable to its depositors, not to shareholders looking to maximize profits. Because of that accountability to depositors, the mutual bank structure also protects the mission of the bank in a way Charley thought conventional shareholder ownership would not.

Until Walden Mutual, the most recently chartered new mutual bank was Volunteer Federal Savings Bank, which opened its doors in 1973 in Madisonville, Tennessee. For many decades, banking regulators and policy makers got caught up in an ideological backlash against the mutual bank model, fueled by the idea that all companies, including banks, were better off putting profits for shareholders before all else. When Charley was opening Walden Mutual, no one involved in approving new bank applications at the New Hampshire Banking Department or the Federal Deposit Insurance Corporation had any experience with reviewing an application from a mutual bank, and both agencies had to sign off before the bank could open for business. The main issue for state and federal banking regulators was that, since 1973, banking regulations have changed significantly, especially after the financial crisis that started in late 2007. Regulators today require banks to have much higher capital than required previously. Because mutual banks don't have conventional shareholders, they can't call upon them to boost capital levels when needed. That can mean running into difficulty maintaining required capital levels, leading many mutual banks over the years to convert into conventional shareholder-owned banks. For a prospective new mutual bank, it wasn't clear if it would be able to raise enough startup capital to comply with modern capital requirements. It took more than the usual amount of convincing just to give Walden Mutual the chance to find startup investors who would be willing to limit their own returns so that the bank could retain enough earnings to stay in compliance.

As it turned out, the two things that might have separately lowered the chances of Walden Mutual ever opening for business—its ownership structure and its mission—actually ended up feeding into each other as strengths to get through the application process and raise the startup capital for the bank. Having a clear social mission protected by a mutual structure was a big draw for the growing number of investors looking to invest with social and environmental impact in mind. With its funky structure as a selling point, Walden Mutual was able to raise $25 million in so-called special deposits from those investors to use as startup capital. These deposits are not insured by the FDIC, and they can't be sold for a higher price later like stock shares can, but each special deposit account does accrue a share of the bank's profits on an annual basis.

Both investors and regulators were also convinced that the bank's board and management had sufficient experience and relationships in sustainable farming, food production, and retail to be able to assess potential borrowers and underwrite loans successfully in this growing niche.

Besides Charley's experience running a sustainable meat company, several board members have experience working in and or doing business with organic farmers or local food companies—including board chair Vince Siciliano, formerly of New Resource Bank. It was also important that others on the bank's proposed executive team include people with experience in banking generally, beyond local or organic foods. The team came together through social networks, including many whom Charley didn't know until after he started organizing the bank. Some of the initial management team came from other mutual banks nearby.

It would have been a lot less red tape to simply start some kind of nonbank investment fund, pooling capital from a bunch of wealthy families, foundations, corporations, or large banks and turning around to make loans to farmers and other food businesses in the supply chain. And there are such funds that can work with new or early-stage businesses that are too new for any bank to work with, even Walden Mutual. Just another investment fund would be insufficient to scale up the sustainable food ecosystem, however. At some point, businesses just need a bank loan, which means that they need a bank that has built up its own internal knowledge to understand their industry and their business model so that it can make them a loan on terms that only a lender that holds federally insured deposits can match.

If you are in the business of making loans, no other funding source can match the combination of abundance and affordability of federally insured deposits. Banks in the United States held around $19 trillion in deposits as of March 2024.[7] Since federal insurance covers around $11 trillion of that, the majority of deposits are virtually risk-free, which means that banks pay less in interest on those deposits than any other source of funding any other financial institution has. That's a big reason big banks are so hungry to keep pulling in everyone's deposits—the relatively low cost of deposits provides a massive boost to their profitability while also giving them flexibility to structure affordable loan products for their favored clients. Walden Mutual Bank, Climate First Bank, and Clean Energy Credit Union are just trying to bring some of that lending flexibility and affordability to their clients.

Chapter 6

Tilting the Landscape Back Where We Need It

When New Deal–era policy makers decided that they wanted to encourage and allow millions of families to acquire single-family homes using thirty-year fixed rate mortgages, they did it using a scheme that worked through community banks and credit unions. First, the lenders made the loans to developers to build the homes; then, the lenders provided households with the thirty-year mortgages to buy the homes. Extending the loans out to thirty years made the monthly payments affordable to the average household—but it was a big risk to the lenders. That's why these thirty-year mortgages were backed by federal mortgage insurance from the Federal Housing Administration (FHA) and could be sold after origination to the Federal National Mortgage Association, better known as Fannie Mae, the government-sponsored enterprise created as part of the New Deal to support home mortgage lending nationwide. Selling the loans to Fannie Mae freed up each lender to do many more loans than it would if it had to wait thirty years for the loans to be repaid—but the loans would still be serviced by the private lenders, meaning that the repayments and relationships for borrowers would still be with their community bank or credit union. This scheme worked on a scale nobody had ever seen before. From 1934 to 1962, community banks and credit unions made

$120 billion in FHA-insured home mortgages that they sold to Fannie Mae.[1] Unfortunately, New Deal–era policy makers also baked redlining into the FHA and Fannie Mae underwriting guidelines for community lenders, so more than 98 percent of those dollars went to White homebuyers to purchase homes in White-only communities.[2] Looking back, it was also clearly not the greatest idea to focus all that lending to build up suburban-style, car-centric communities. Despite these significant shortcomings, it's another example of how, with intentional support from the public sector, locally owned and locally controlled financial institutions can play a key role collectively doing big things. The challenge now is figuring out what kinds of support from the public sector could serve the goal of tilting the landscape back in favor of community banking institutions, after decades of tilting the other way.

Reclaiming Deposit Insurance

Of all the ways the public sector has supported community banking, one of the most transformative was deposit insurance, which protects community banks' access to stable, reliable, and low-cost deposits as a source of funding. The way deposit insurance generally works is that the participating banks contribute to a central pot of money, the deposit insurance fund, and when one or more banks fail, the fund pays out what's owed to depositors. There's usually a cap on the deposit amount covered per depositor. Since 2008, federal deposit insurance has covered up to $250,000 per depositor, per account type, per bank or credit union. The thinking around the insurance cap is twofold. First, it limits the potential hit to the fund in case it has to pay out. Second, the idea is that the average person or business owner with a bank account doesn't have the time or the skill to accurately assess whether their deposits are safe in one bank versus another, whereas wealthier account holders or larger businesses do have the time and resources to make those assessments themselves. That's why the agency managing the deposit insurance fund is also typically charged with regularly examining each participating bank to ensure safe and sound lending practices, guarding against the risk that the fund might have to pay out more than what it might have in its coffers and theoretically performing that due diligence function on behalf of the bank account holders who don't have the time or resources to do it for themselves.

Before deposit insurance, the first sign of trouble would send everyone running to withdraw their money from their bank—the phenomenon known as a bank run. Bank runs themselves were often the cause of a bank failure, turning rumors into self-fulfilling prophecies. In 1829, seeking to stabilize its growing banking sector, already the largest and wealthiest in the young nation, New York became the first state to institute its own bank deposit insurance program. Larger banks opposed the creation of deposit insurance, seeing it as unnecessary and costly since banks themselves pay ongoing deposit insurance assessments based on a percentage of their assets, meaning that larger banks pay higher assessments.[3] Between 1829 and 1863, five other states—Vermont, Indiana, Michigan, Ohio, and Iowa—followed New York with deposit insurance programs of their own, and—with the exception of Michigan—they proved to be a success in terms of stabilizing community banks and allowing them to finance the growth of bustling new manufacturing towns, especially along the Erie Canal and the Great Lakes shipping route all the way to Chicago.[4]

Between 1907 and 1917, another eight states created deposit insurance programs—Oklahoma, Kansas, Nebraska, Texas, Mississippi, South Dakota, North Dakota, and Washington—although they were not as successful.[5] During the boom years of the Roaring Twenties, an average of 635 banks failed every year across the United States.[6] From 1929 to 1933, in the early years of the Great Depression, more than nine thousand banks failed, including many larger banks.[7] Although President Franklin Delano Roosevelt often gets credited for creating federal deposit insurance as part of the New Deal, he actually opposed its creation until the last minute. Legislators from the Midwest and South, led by US Representative Henry Steagall from Alabama, finally won him over[8]—and that was only after it became clear everything else President Roosevelt had tried to stabilize the banking system turned out to be not enough. Federal deposit insurance went into effect on January 1, 1934, providing bank depositors with up to $2,500 in deposit insurance coverage, a threshold that has gone up over time. The impact was immediate, as only nine banks failed in 1934. Since federal deposit insurance went into effect, no depositor has ever lost a single penny of federally insured deposits in the United States. Between 1941 and 1979, an average of only 5.3 banks failed a year.[9]

In 2023, the sudden failures of Silicon Valley Bank and Signature Bank were notable because, at the time they failed, each bank had an unusually high percentage of uninsured deposits—meaning deposits in accounts holding far beyond the $250,000 deposit insurance limit. At most banks, 40 to 60 percent of their deposits are above the deposit insurance limit, largely because many businesses and also government entities need to keep millions in their accounts on a daily basis just for cash flow reasons, such as making payroll. Due to their particular client bases and business models, Silicon Valley Bank and Signature Bank both had more than 90 percent uninsured deposits. When their clients got spooked because of potential loses at either bank, classic bank runs ensued. But federal banking regulators have become very good at protecting all deposits, not just insured deposits. It's actually very rare that federal regulators actually pay out to insured depositors when a bank fails. Out of 3,622 bank failures since 1970, in only 288 instances did federal bank regulators actually pay out insured deposit amounts to depositors.[10] The most common outcome, in 2,154 of those failures, all or most of the deposits—including uninsured deposits—were simply moved into accounts at another bank.[11] That's what eventually happened in the case of both Silicon Valley Bank and Signature Bank, as well as all three other banks that failed in 2023.[12]

Meanwhile, amid the chaotic headlines and coverage around those bank failures in 2023, any reports of community banks' demise as a result of those prominent bank failures were greatly exaggerated. Although it was true that, in the aftermath of the early March 2023 bank failures, many depositors were moving to larger banks, those were mostly big depositors of midsize or large regional banks moving uninsured deposits to even larger banks based on the perception that federal regulators considered those largest banks to be "too big to fail." Although some reports labeled Silicon Valley Bank or Signature Bank as small banks, because they were much smaller than any of the big four banks, Silicon Valley Bank was the sixteenth largest bank in the United States at the time of its collapse, and Signature Bank was ranked twenty-ninth.[13] Community banks, on the other hand, were able to hold steady, benefiting from both close ties to their customers as well as the continued power of federal deposit insurance. As of December 31, 2022, community banks across the country collectively held $2.3 trillion in deposits.[14] By March 31, 2024, just a few weeks after Silicon Valley Bank and Signature Bank's failures, community banks held almost the exact same $2.3 trillion in deposits.[15] A year after that, there was still basically the same amount of deposits held at community banks across the country.[16]

That doesn't mean that nothing has to change about federal deposit insurance. Ironically, the FDIC today shoulders a lot of responsibility for the banking consolidation that's occurred since the 1980s. It gets to approve or deny bank merger applications, and since 2013, it has approved 1,251 merger applications while denying none.[17] It's also had a hand in the dramatic drop-off in new bank formation. Banks can't open for business anymore without first getting approved for federal deposit insurance. In the decade prior to the financial crisis of 2007–2009, an average of 153 new banks opened for business across the United States every year. Between 2010 and 2023, fewer than 100 new banks opened their doors—most of them since 2019. One big reason for that drop-off is the dramatically higher amount in startup capital that's generally required for new banks today versus before the crisis.[18] It's higher in part because the operating costs of banks have risen, between the costs of staffing as well as technology and the costs of compliance with antimoney laundering and fraud prevention rules. But it's also higher because regulators have come to believe higher capital requirements make for a more stable banking system, reducing the chances that the FDIC will have to deal with another big wave of bank failures. The FDIC has the most influence over the amount in startup capital required for each prospective new bank to raise before it opens for business. The exact required amount can differ based on the target market of the bank and the intended business model, but the generally expected number as of 2022 was approximately $20 million.[19] That's what prospective banks need to raise up front to cover their first three years of operations while also keeping up with regulatory capital requirements over the course of those three years. One idea floating around is that maybe new banks don't need to raise all their required capital before they open their doors, instead allowing the flexibility for new banks to raise some of the required amount within the first three years after they open.

From another perspective, there's an argument to be made for lower capital requirements. There were many decades, from the 1940s to the 1970s, and even the 1990s, when capital requirements were not as high or as stringent as they are today, yet bank failures were very rare and new bank charters were much more frequent. It's possible, although it's hard to determine at this point, whether the current prevailing approach to capital requirements is costing too much in terms of slowing down the creation of new community banks for the sake of preventing bank failures that aren't as likely to happen as regulators seem to think it is. In years or decades when there isn't a financial crisis, bank failures are extremely rare, especially given the number of banks that exist, even today after decades of bank consolidation. It's as if the FDIC itself is underestimating the power of its main function, which is to provide the deposit insurance that virtually eliminated bank runs from its very inception and made it possible for community banks to form and thrive across the country. Although global megabanks may need significantly higher capital levels to ensure their stability while making esoteric, complex and risky investments that only they are willing and able to make, community banks are still mostly doing what their communities have always needed them to do—the very boring things like mortgages, commercial real estate loans, and small business loans. Higher capital requirements make it more difficult to form new community banks to bring those boring things to places that have long been denied access to them, places that shouldn't have to wait for big banks or protest for big banks to work with them.

Reclaiming Public Ownership

Keeping up with capital requirements is also a huge challenge over the life of a banking institution, especially if its ownership or management comes from communities that have faced generational barriers to creating wealth. It's not just about the startup phase. One of the biggest components of bank and credit union regulations is the amount of regulatory capital that institutions are required to hold on their balance sheets at all times as a cushion against losses. As a reminder—although the exact ratios these days are based on much more complicated formulas—banks have to have around $1 in regulatory capital for every $12 in assets on their balance sheets, and credit unions have to have $1 in regulatory capital (which credit unions call "net worth") for every $16 in assets in their balance sheets. For banks, the initial amount comes from their startup investors; for credit unions, initial regulatory capital comes as a donation from the sponsor entity, which can be a church, a company, a local union chapter, or maybe a nonprofit.

Over time, banks and credit unions can grow their balance sheets by retaining some of their net earnings as regulatory capital. Banks can also grow by issuing new ownership shares to their stockholders, or credit unions can raise new donations from their sponsor entities. There are also ways for banks or credit unions to borrow funds that they can use temporarily as part of their regulatory capital. Capital requirement ratios have also changed and evolved over time. In the United States' early days, each institution would negotiate their capital requirement ratio with the legislatures that chartered them. Today, there are industry-wide standard capital requirements set by bank and credit union regulators, and the formulas they use are also subject to change over time. One consequence coming out of the prolonged savings and loan crisis of the 1980s was a gradual increase in the amounts and a decrease in the flexibility around capital requirements. Stung by the thousands of bank failures, regulators began to require more regulatory capital. Bank regulators also started using formulas applied uniformly across all banks whereas before they would set capital requirements uniquely for each bank based on its track record and other factors specific to each bank. Many community banks merged with each other or with larger institutions because larger institutions could more easily attract shareholders by offering more in profits to distribute as dividends every quarter. The elimination of geographic restrictions on banks cleared the path for more and more consolidation. If a bank has a rough year and the losses eat up some of its capital, regulators may require it to formulate a plan to raise capital from shareholders to get its ratio back in compliance. That plan may involve merging with another institution, which is what happened, for example, to Consolidated Bank and Trust in 2005 (see chapter 1).

Ponce Bank won't have to worry about its capital requirements for a while. Its largest shareholder today is the US Treasury, which in 2022 took out a $225 million nonvoting ownership stake in the bank.[20] The investment was part of the Emergency Capital Investment Program (ECIP), created as part of the federal government's response to the COVID-19 pandemic and its economic fallout. Under ECIP, the US Treasury invested a total of $8.4 billion in ninety-one banks and eighty-three credit unions, all of them federally certified CDFIs, minority-designated depository institutions, or both.[21] Ponce Bank was one of the larger recipients, but at the other end of the scale, New Covenant Dominion Federal Credit Union also received an ECIP investment of just $148,000. Crucially, the investments were structured to serve as regulatory capital for each institution, allowing each to scale up significantly as a result of the investment without having to worry about raising capital from shareholders or cash-strapped donors in the case of credit unions serving low- to moderate-income communities.

ECIP investments also came on terms that are better than most private investors would ever take. ECIP recipients don't have to pay any dividends to the US Treasury for two years; after that, the dividend will be based on how much lending the bank provides to borrowers of color, low- and moderate-income borrowers, or businesses in low- to moderate-income neighborhoods. The more a bank can lend to these communities, the lower its dividend payment rate will be, ranging from 0.5 percent to 2 percent. Although ECIP is technically a one-shot deal, if it's successful, it could become a template for some version of it to become an ongoing way for the federal government to protect and encourage local control of the banking system while accommodating the need for higher capital requirements as a way to stabilize the banking system.

The idea of the public sector partially or even fully owning banks may seem anathema today after decades of private-sector driven policy that started in the 1980s during the Ronald Reagan administration and continued under presidents of both parties, but it's actually how banking first took root in the United States. After the ratification of the Constitution took away the power of states to tax imports and exports, one of the main ways states sought to generate revenue was through dividends from partial or even total ownership of banks. In the earliest days of the new republic, private bank investors needed approval directly from state legislatures to obtain bank charters, and often part of the agreement was the state would take an ownership stake in a new bank. Pennsylvania, South Carolina, Kentucky, and Tennessee dabbled in partial or full state ownership of banks. The Bank of Pennsylvania, with the state owning one-third of its shares, served as the depository of all state government revenues. States in the South and West tended to require chartered banks to finance infrastructure development. Over time, the public sector's purview over banks, as shareholders or as chartering entities, has faded away into an afterthought. Banking industry lobbyists, not to mention economics departments and a lot of business journalists, have slowly but surely chipped away at the notion that the public should have any power over, let alone ownership of, banks—except for one place: North Dakota.

The State-Owned Bank of North Dakota

Fowzia Adde arrived in the United States in the late 1990s as a nineteen-year-old refugee from Somalia, landing alone in Washington, DC. Her mother, father, and siblings arrived a few months later. Fowzia found work as a convenience store cashier and housekeeper. She managed to keep in touch with the friends she had made in her refugee camp prior to being resettled in the United States, and they ended up being resettled in Fargo, North Dakota. She found out that they were paying a lot less in rent and other living expenses than she was, so she decided to join them. In Fargo, she found work in a wire factory, making components for motorcycles. By 2002, however, she was one of a dozen people from Somalia, Latin America, Vietnam, or the Middle East who were unhappy working on the same production line in what felt like dead-end jobs. Like so many immigrants before and since, they wanted to start their own businesses. In 2003, after talking about it on work breaks and weekend meetings, the group founded the Immigrant Development Center to help new arrivals like themselves and others in and around Fargo start new businesses. Fowzia became the executive director.

One day in 2018, a pair of business partners came into Fowzia's office, one originally from Iraq and one from Jordan. They owned a grocery store in Fargo called F-M International Foods, and they wanted a loan to buy the building they were renting for their business. Fowzia helped the pair draft a business plan to obtain a loan for $250,000 from Corner-stone Bank, a community bank based in Fargo. She's built a great work-ing relationship with Cornerstone, working with one or two clients a year on getting small business loans from the bank. Little did she or any of those clients realize that, behind the scenes, a portion of each small busi-ness loan actually came from the state-owned Bank of North Dakota, a unique institution created in 1919 as a way to support local economic development across the state.

The Bank of North Dakota was the last remaining state-owned bank until 2016, when it was joined by the Territorial Bank of American Samoa. Prohibited by law from competing with the private sector, the Bank of North Dakota has no branches, and it doesn't issue debit cards or credit cards. To open an account as an individual or business at the bank, you have to go in person to the bank's headquarters in the state capital of Bismarck, and you have to have a North Dakota state-issued ID or driver's license. Rather than the Bank of North Dakota relying on individuals or private businesses for deposits, the state government of North Dakota is required by law to deposit all its taxes, fees, and other revenues into the state-owned bank. As a result, almost 90 percent of the Bank of North Dakota's deposits come from the state, not from individual or business accounts.

Other than student loans, people or businesses generally don't apply for loans directly from the Bank of North Dakota. The vast majority of the bank's lending happens through loan participations. In a loan par-ticipation, the loan originator covers part of the borrowed amount and then it brings in other lenders behind the scenes to cover the rest, and everyone shares in the interest paid on the loan. It's not uncommon for private lenders to do loan participations with each other, especially on larger loans. It's a way for lenders to share risk. But it's unusual to see private banks buying and selling loan participations for loans as small as $250,000 or less. It's not usually worth it for the second institution to participate in loans that small, but that's how Cornerstone Bank worked with the Bank of North Dakota for the loan to F-M International Foods. Loan participations for smaller business loans are just one of the ways the state-owned Bank of North Dakota partners with community banks and credit unions all over the state. It allows local banking institutions to leverage a deeper pool of funding while maintaining their relationships with their clients. Loan participations also help with maintaining capital requirements—by selling participations in their loans to the Bank of North Dakota, community banks and credit unions in North Dakota can manage their balance sheet growth and avoid situations in which they might need to raise new regulatory capital to accommodate sudden growth spurts. In a typical year, the Bank of North Dakota does four hundred to five hundred business loan participations and three hundred to four hundred agriculture loan participations in partnership with private lenders across the state. With the Bank of North Dakota supporting them from behind the scenes, community banks in North Dakota have a higher market share than they do in any other state—78.8 percent.[22]

Recently, campaigns to create more state-, city-, or county-owned banks modeled after the Bank of North Dakota have emerged in places that could not be more different than North Dakota in terms of geography, demographics, or politics. In California, a grassroots coalition of environmental and racial justice groups and labor groups got a bill passed at the state level in 2019 to enable local governments in the state to charter their own banks. Groups in San Francisco and other parts of the Bay Area as well as Los Angeles have been working with local legislators to take advantage of the opportunity. Legislators and advocates in New York State have been working since 2019 to pass a similar bill. In 2022, Philadelphia City Council passed a bill creating a new quasi-government entity charged with creating a city-owned bank.

During the pandemic, some communities got a small sample of what it might be like to work with a public bank doing loan participations with community banks and credit unions. As part of the federal government's COVID-19 response in 2020, the Federal Reserve System created a temporary loan participation program to provide cheap credit for otherwise healthy businesses to survive the worst of the pandemic. Called the Main Street Lending Program, it involved the Federal Reserve system itself purchasing loan participations from local lenders across the United States. The program was only open for the last six months of 2020, but as Samira Rajan, CEO of Brooklyn Cooperative Federal Credit Union from chapter 2, told me, it allowed her credit union to make several loans beyond its usual lending limits to local Brooklyn businesses, including an urban planning firm and a multivehicle food truck business. Without the Federal Reserve purchasing those loan participations, "we wouldn't have been able to do those loans," Samira told me. "They would have been turned away."

Melissa Marquez inherited her mother's deep desire to make the banking system work for those whom it has long excluded. At age fourteen, she saw her mother break down in tears again and again after coming home from work as a loan officer at a bank. The bank refused to lend to their community in Barrio Logan, an epicenter of Chicano culture in San Diego, her mother told her. Barrio Logan residents would come in, make their deposits, and stay faithful customers to the bank, but still couldn't get access to credit. That memory from 1974 drove Melissa to help spearhead a coalition of tenant organizers, community groups, and elected officials that have spent the last few years calling for more government-owned banks across New York.

Melissa has tried every other approach in her forty-plus years of working in community development, the last twenty of them with Genesee Co-op Federal Credit Union in Rochester, New York, where she is currently CEO. Opened in 1982, Genesee Co-op serves forty-two hundred members in the city's diverse, working-class "South Wedge" neighborhoods—the former stomping grounds of abolitionist icon Frederick Douglass and jazz legend Cab Calloway. But for all that Melissa has been able to do at Genesee Co-op, providing credit to the kinds of communities that her mother ached to serve, it still pales in comparison to the credit and investment needs that she encounters daily in Greater Rochester's working-class neighborhoods. Even after forty years of growth, Genesee Co-op today has just $40 million in assets.

"The scale that's needed is more than we can do by ourselves," Melissa told me. "All along, the idea of who can that partner be has been in my mind."

In 2024, Melissa joined Rochester's mayor, city council members, and its state legislators in a last-minute push for state legislation to create a "public bank" called the Bank of Rochester. They envision a government-owned financial institution built specifically to hold only government deposits while partnering with local private lenders like Genesee Co-op to boost their ability to make loans and investments in communities that still aren't getting enough of it. The Bank of Rochester would be modeled largely after the Bank of North Dakota. Individuals or businesses wouldn't be able to open accounts at the proposed Bank of Rochester. Rather, it would be authorized to take deposits only from government bodies, including local or state government as well as federal offices. Restricting a public bank to government deposits limits the public bank from competing with private institutions for deposits from individuals or businesses. According to the City of Rochester's most recent annual financial report, the municipal government had nearly $500 million on deposit in various accounts at private banks. The Bank of Rochester wouldn't immediately take in all those deposits—the legislation authorizes the chief financial officers of both Rochester and the surrounding Monroe County to add the Bank of Rochester to their rosters of banks approved to hold deposits from the city or county government.

Like its counterpart in North Dakota, the Bank of Rochester's lending would be primarily wholesale lending—loans to other financial institutions—or loan participations. That means that the public bank would rely on the existing expertise of local lenders and their relationships with their communities to underwrite loans, while local lenders could access a deeper pool of funds to support their lending. Loan participations also help guard against corruption. There's plenty of concern and criticism around state-owned or local government-owned banks, and often one of the first to come up is how to guard against corruption and political favoritism in loan decisions at an institution controlled even indirectly by elected officials. But community banks and credit unions are all highly regulated themselves, meaning that their regulators examine their lending practices and management on an ongoing basis to ensure safe and sound operations, which includes guarding against political influence in lending decisions.

Melissa has also tried the Community Reinvestment Act route. She cofounded the Greater Rochester Community Reinvestment Coalition back in 1993 as a vehicle to hold banks accountable for the legal obligation to serve all communities regardless of race or income level. But there just hasn't been enough interest from other private lenders to participate in the loans that Genesee Co-op makes. Part of the challenge is the complicated process of reconciling different lending standards across different institutions, especially when many loan participations could be for loans of less than $100,000—far below typical thresholds for loan participations with mainstream banking institutions. Genesee Co-op also generally uses lending standards that go beyond the flexibility other lenders are willing to provide.

"If they wanted to do it, they would have already been doing it for years by now," Melissa told me. "The Bank of Rochester would have it written into its mandate to do these kinds of loan participations that support access to credit in the communities we serve, who have long been denied that access."

Melissa said that she believes that a Bank of Rochester's presence in the market would help draw in other local lenders into providing more loans and investments in the South Wedge and other historically disinvested areas around Rochester, with or without any direct involvement from her credit union. She also believes that a local public bank could influence prevailing lending practices by only offering to participate in loans that use nonpredatory terms and interest rates, particularly when it comes to car loans.

New York pioneered deposit insurance in the United States, more than a century before the advent of federal deposit insurance. Deposit insurance helped community banks play a key role in the early economic development of the state, complementing the larger public investment of the Erie Canal. There were many towns and cities along the canal, but it was the towns and cities where local leaders obtained a bank charter that grew the quickest and the most.[23] Rochester became one of the largest of them all. Melissa hopes that New York can once again take up the mantle of using creative, unorthodox public policy to support a more well-functioning banking system—one that finally honors her mother's aspirations.

Conclusion

For as long as recorded human history, communities have created their own banking institutions as a way to solve problems. It's a part of our story as a species. Human beings are social animals driven by complex and sophisticated relationships, including credit and banking relationships. That's why reclaiming community banking is about more than just access to credit. It's also about the measure of economic self-determination that comes from a community having the ability to extend credit based on relationships—based on our belief in one another. The injustice of disinvestment isn't just about the lack of capital flowing to certain communities. It's also about how the whole system undermined the ability of those communities to wield at least some of their own power to influence the flows of credit and capital.

The scale of today's challenges—yawning and persistent racial wealth gaps, the ever-rising cost of housing, and climate change—can make it seem like only the big banks have the necessary scale to meet the moment. As much as big banks can and should do to help, however, the United States is no exception to the part of the human story where locally owned and locally controlled banking institutions play a key role in responding to big challenges. They played a key role in building cities and towns, they played a key role in building the suburbs (which wasn't entirely a good thing but it was a big thing), and they still play key roles in main-taining and financing local businesses. But they haven't done big things on their own, and community banking institutions have always needed support from public policy instruments like federal deposit insurance, Fannie Mae, and even the institution of government-backed money in the form of deposits, not just cash.

Hardly anyone these days—not even bankers themselves—really talks about how banks have the power to create new money. Most bankers would say something along the lines of "We're in the business of taking deposits and making loans," which is technically a correct statement, but the precise relationship is not very obvious. I'll always remember learning about "fractional reserve" banking in my introductory macro-economics class. The lesson went something like this: Someone deposits $100 into a hypothetical bank, but the bank is only required to "keep" 10 percent in reserves while lending out the other $90 to the next person. That next person gets the $90 deposited in their account, and the bank now only needs to keep $9 in reserves while lending out the $81 to the next person. The pattern repeats until there's basically nothing left to lend out. At that time, about seventy people will end up with a cumula-tive total of nearly $1,000 deposited in their accounts and will owe the bank the same amount plus interest, while the bank will have around $100 in reserves. If everyone runs to the bank to withdraw their deposits all at once, they'll demand the $1,000 in cash, and the bank fails because it only has $100 in cash reserves—hence the phrase "fractional reserve" banking. Fractional reserve banking implied that the entire economy is constantly teetering on the edge of oblivion. It's why bank runs became a thing in the first place: once people lost faith in their bank, they ran to withdraw their deposits, and the banks never had enough currency (or gold) to meet all the withdrawal requests coming in at once.

Like many stories economics professors use to explain how things work or how they came to be that way, the fractional reserve story isn't quite the complete and accurate picture of what's really happening in the real world, but it's useful for getting across the basics of how banks create new money whenever they make a loan. After the first person deposits their $100 and the bank loans out $90 to the next person, it's not as though the first person's account balance drops to $10. That $100 is still right where they left it in their account, available to spend as they please—even after the bank has made the $90 loan to the next person. The same holds true after the bank makes the $81 loan to the third person, and so on. If these seventy people or businesses only do business with one another and all the money stays deposited in the bank at the end of each transaction, all they'll be doing is shifting around the $1,000 in deposits to and from one another's accounts. That's $1,000 floating around this hypothetical economy that started out with just $100 deposited in one account that got turned into $1,000 in deposits through the process of the bank making loans. Economists sometimes call it "checkbook money." Most money out in the world today has never existed as currency; rather, it has only ever existed as checkbook money, created initially by banks whenever they make a loan.

The money creation power of banks was much more obvious in the United States' early days. Although there was some wealth floating around the US economy at the time in the form of gold, silver, or foreign currency, there certainly wasn't enough to invest in the building of a new country, and, unsurprisingly, most of that wealth ended up in the hands of those who were already well-off. The first community banks emerged as a solution to the problem, with states chartering local institutions with the power to print new money and lend it out to people and businesses. When a bank made a loan, it printed its own bank notes that people and businesses began using and circulating locally. Banks and businesses in one town or city would generally recognize and accept notes printed by nearby banks, and the banks would settle with each other by exchanging currencies back to their originators. From 1793 to 1861, about sixteen hundred private banks across the United States were licensed to print and circulate their own paper currency under state-granted bank charters.[1]

It was just as chaotic as it sounds. To facilitate business further afield, newspapers published bank note tables and publishers sold subscriptions for regional and national bank note catalogs containing images, descriptions, and exchange rates for private bank-issued currencies across the United States, allowing banks and business owners to detect counterfeits and also devalue certain currencies if news circulated that certain banks were making risky loans—not to mention verifying if the bank printed on the note was still in business or if it ever really existed in the first place. As chaotic as this nationwide patchwork of paper currencies was, it served the public purpose of building communities where people could live, work, gather, and play. Granted, it was all on stolen land, and a lot of it was cultivated or built using stolen labor.

It took more than a hundred years, from New York's first state deposit insurance program in 1829 to 1933, for the federal government to finally extend deposit insurance on a nationwide scale. By practically eliminating bank runs as a constant cause of bank failure, federal deposit insurance helped preserve and stabilize community banks as a source of money creation in the form of checkbook money. Even though banks no longer issue their own currencies, they still create new money in the same way every time they make a loan. As alternatives emerged like mutual banks or savings and loan associations and minority-owned banks or credit unions, it took time and political organizing work, but policy makers came to recognize them and even encouraged their proliferation across the United States in parallel with traditional local banks. Policy makers even expanded federal deposit insurance to savings and loan associations and, in 1970, to credit unions. Gradually, all these alternatives have come to be more and more like banks—which has some downsides too—in that they all gained the power to create new checkbook money whenever they make a loan.

By 2023, a working paper from the Federal Reserve Bank of Philadelphia stated it this way: "Private money creation by banks enables lending to not be constrained by the supply of cash deposits. During the 2001–2020 period, 92 percent of bank deposits were due to funding liquidity creation, and during 2011–2020 funding liquidity creation averaged $10.7 trillion per year, or 57 percent of [gross domestic product]."[2] In other words, from 2011 to 2020, banks created $10.7 trillion in deposits every year, all out of thin air. Today that power gets taken completely for granted, and it's becoming increasingly concentrated in a few large global megabanks.

Back in 1984, localized money creation power was deployed across 15,767 community banks[3] and more than 15,000 credit unions[4] across the United States. By 2024, localized money creation power was reduced to just 4,128 community banks[5] and fewer than 4,600 credit unions.[6]

Money creation power is still intentionally and structurally limited to just 124 community banks and approximately 500 credit unions owned or controlled by and primarily serving communities of color, communities soon to represent the majority of the population. Due to the way federal banking agencies currently regulate the bank chartering process, even White communities today have more difficulty than ever chartering a new community bank and thereby gaining new local power to create money to meet their needs. And, whether it's lack of imagination or lack of exposure or just willful disregard for the environment, those who wield the most power to create money today remain limited in their ability to transition communities away from carbon-based energy.

In the meantime, the big global megabanks that control more and more of the banking system are able to use that money creation power to continue funding war, prisons, the gun industry, fossil fuels, and private equity funds that are ravaging industries from real estate to journalism to healthcare and education. The four largest US banks are also the four biggest financers of the fossil fuel industry worldwide—Chase, Citi, Wells Fargo, and Bank of America.[7]

Reclaiming community banking isn't just about opening up access to credit and banking to people and places that never had the same level of access or no longer have it. It's not just about investing in new technologies, building methods and materials that are environmentally responsible. It's not about redistributing wealth from those who have to those from whom it's been stolen—that's something worth doing on its own, and community banking institutions can be part of it, but there's more to community banking than that. Reclaiming community banking is about redistributing—or in some cases restoring—the secret superpower of money creation to the communities we are today so that each community can leverage its relationships as part of responding to the challenges confronting us all. Challenges like transitioning to renewable energy or more sustainable food production or building housing that the average household can actually afford, creating a new locally owned grocery store down the street—or preserving the grocery that's served the neighborhood for decades.

Notes

Introduction

1. Loren Henderson et al., "Credit Where Credit Is Due? Race, Gender, and Discrimination in the Credit Scores of Business Startups," *Review of Black Political Economy* 42 (June 2015), 459–79.
2. Federal Deposit Insurance Corporation, FDIC Quarterly Banking Profile, "Ratios for Community and Noncommunity Banks," accessed November 6, 2023. https://www.fdic.gov/analysis/quarterly-banking-profile/index.html.
3. Federal Deposit Insurance Corporation, FDIC Quarterly Banking Profile, "Ratios."
4. Drew Desilver, "Most U.S. Bank Failures Have Come in a Few Big Waves," Pew Research Center, April 11, 2023. https://www.pewresearch.org/short-reads/2023/04/11/most-u-s-bank-failures-have-come-in-a-few-big-waves/.
5. Desilver, "Most U.S. Bank Failures."
6. Desilver, "Most U.S. Bank Failures."
7. David Mengle, "The Case for Interstate Branch Banking," *FRB Richmond Economic Review* 76, no. 6 (November/December 1990): 3–17. https://ssrn.com/abstract=2122684.
8. Federal Financial Institutions Examination Council, Reports of Condition and Income, March 31, 2024.

9. Federal Financial Institutions Examination Council, Reports of Condition and Income.

10. US Small Business Administration Office of Advocacy, "Frequently Asked Questions about Small Business," March 7, 2023. https://advocacy.sba.gov/2023/03/07/frequently-asked-questions-about-small-business-2023/.

11. Federal Financial Institutions Examination Council, Reports of Condition and Income, December 31, 2023.

12. Federal Reserve Banks, "2024 Report on Employer Firms: Findings from the 2023 Small Business Credit Survey," *Small Business Credit Survey*, March 7, 2024. https://doi.org/10.55350/sbcs-20240307.

13. These figures are calculated using the overall loan-to-asset ratio for community banks. Taking 39 percent of total assets in the banking industry, or $9 trillion, if community banks represented that amount of assets with the same loan-to-asset ratio, they would have $6 trillion in loans in their portfolios, or roughly 3.3 times what existing community banks currently hold on their balance sheets. Multiplying relevant portfolio line items for existing community bank assets by 3.3 and subtracting the current total for each line item leaves the difference being the amount by which each line item would be higher if community banks were 39 percent instead of 11 percent of the banking industry today.

14. Federal Reserve Banks, "2022 Report on Firms Owned by People of Color: Based on the 2021 Small Business Credit Survey," *Small Business Credit Survey*, June 29, 2022. https://doi.org/10.55350/sbcs-20220629.

15. Howard Bodenhorn and David Cuberes, "Finance and Urbanization in Early Nineteenth-Century New York," *Journal of Urban Economics* 104 (2018): 47–58. https://doi.org/10.1016/j.jue.2018.01.001.

16. Bodenhorn and Cuberes, "Finance and Urbanization."

17. Aditya Aladangady, Andrew C. Chang, and Jacob Krimmel, "Greater Wealth, Greater Uncertainty: Changes in Racial Inequality in the Survey of Consumer Finances," *FEDS Notes* (Washington, DC: Board of Governors of the Federal Reserve System, October 18, 2023). https://doi.org/10.17016/2380-7172.3405.

18. This point is a major takeaway from banking historian and law professor Mehrsa Baradaran's book *The Color of Money: Black Banks and the Racial Wealth Gap* (Cambridge, MA: Belknap Press of Harvard University Press, 2017).

19. This point is a major takeaway from race scholar Keeanga-Yamahtta Taylor's book *Race for Profit: How Banks and the Real Estate Industry Undermined Black Homeownership* (Chapel Hill: University of North Carolina Press, 2019).

20. Author's own analysis of FDIC historical bank data. Last accessed July 13, 2024. https://banks.data.fdic.gov/bankfind-suite/historical.

21. Benjamin Bromberg, "The Origin of Banking: Religious Finance in Babylonia," *Journal of Economic History* 2, no. 1 (1942): 77–88. http://www.jstor.org/stable/2113028.

22. Steven J. Garfinkle, "Shepherds, Merchants, and Credit: Some Observations on Lending Practices in Ur III Mesopotamia," *Journal of the Economic and Social History of the Orient* 47, no. 1 (2004): 1–30. http://www.jstor.org/stable/25165020.

23. Kenneth K. S. Ch'en, "The Role of Buddhist Monasteries in T'ang Society," *History of Religions* 15, no. 3 (1976): 209–30. http://www.jstor.org/stable/1062525.

Chapter 1. For Us, by Us: Minority-Owned Community Banks and Credit Unions

1. Based on author's analysis of New York State Department of Agriculture and Markets database for retail food establishments found at https://data.ny.gov/Economic-Development/Retail-Food-Stores/.

2. Mehrsa Baradaran, *The Color of Money: Black Banks and the Racial Wealth Gap* (Cambridge, MA: Belknap Press of Harvard University Press, 2019).

3. Federal Deposit Insurance Corporation, July 21, 2024. https://banks.data.fdic.gov/bankfind-suite/bankfind.

4. Anthony Barr and Mac McComas, "Minority Depository Institutions: State of Knowledge, Sector Summary and Lending Activity, and Impact, 2010–2022," National Bankers Association and Johns Hopkins University 21st Century Cities Initiative, May 31, 2023. https://www.nationalbankers.org/research-state-of-mdi-report.

5. Anthony Barr et al., "The Social Impact of MDI Mortgage Lending," National Bankers Association, Hip Hop Caucus, and Bank Black USA, June 10, 2024. https://www.nationalbankers.org/the-social-impact-of-mdi-mortgage-lending.

6. Agustin Hurtado and Jung Sakong, "The Effect of Minority Bank Ownership on Minority Credit," George J. Stigler Center for the Study of the Economy and the State Working Paper No. 325, December 5, 2022. https://ssrn.com/abstract=4590142.

7. "2022 Report on Firms Owned by People of Color: Based on the 2021 Small Business Credit Survey," Small Business Credit Survey. Federal Reserve Banks, 2022. https://doi.org/10.55350/sbcs-2022062.

8. US Department of Commerce, Bureau of the Census, Population Estimates Program (PEP), or American Community Survey (ACS). Updated annually.

9. Claire Celerier and Purnoor Tak, "Finance, Advertising, and Race," *Proceedings of the EUROFIDAI-ESSEC Paris December Finance Meeting 2022*, June 17, 2022. http://dx.doi.org/10.2139/ssrn.3825143.

10. Celerier and Tak, "Finance, Advertising, and Race."

11. Celerier and Tak, "Finance, Advertising, and Race."

12. Celerier and Tak, "Finance, Advertising, and Race."

13. John Mullin, "Maggie Lena Walker: How the Daughter of a Former Slave Became a Banking Pioneer," Federal Reserve Bank of Richmond Econ Focus, Fourth Quarter 2022. https://www.richmondfed.org/publications/research/econ_focus/2022/q4_economic_history.

14. Mullin, "Maggie Lena Walker."

15. Committee on Methods and Services, National Association of Mutual Savings Banks, and Thomas H. Riley Jr., "Mutual Savings Banks Cornerstones of American Life 1943" (pamphlet), Book Collections at the Maine State Library 86, 1943. https://digitalmaine.com/books/86.

16. Board of Governors of the Federal Reserve System (U.S.), 1935–, Banking and Monetary Statistics, 1914–1941, 1943, accessed July 21, 2024. https://fraser.stlouisfed.org/title/38; https://fraser.stlouisfed.org/files/docs/publications/bms/1914-1941/BMS14-41_complete.pdf.

17. Board of Governors of the Federal Reserve System, 1943.

18. Federal Deposit Insurance Corporation, "Banker Resource Center: Mutual Institutions," July 18, 2023. Last accessed July 21, 2024. https://www.fdic.gov/resources/bankers/mutual-institutions/index.html.

19. "Puerto Rican Lawyer Sets Up a Savings Concern in the Bronx," *New York Times*, May 3, 1960. https://nyti.ms/43PKmNr.

20. Paul Cromwell, "Welfare Council Named by Mayor," *New York Times*, June 30, 1960. https://nyti.ms/3xkPtsr.

21. US Department of Commerce, Bureau of the Census, *2023 New York City Housing and Vacancy Survey Selected Initial Findings*. https://www.nyc.gov/assets/hpd/downloads/pdfs/about/2023-nychvs-selected-initial-findings.pdf.

22. Federal Financial Institutions Examination Council, data reported under the Home Mortgage Disclosure Act. www.ffiec.gov/hmda.

23. Ponce Financial Group, Inc. *Form 10-K 2023*, Bronx, NY, 2023. https://www.sec.gov/Archives/edgar/data/1874071/000095017024033436/pdlb-20231231.htm.

24. National Credit Union Administration, *1984 Annual Report*, 1984.

25. National Credit Union Administration, *Quarterly Credit Union Data Summary Q1 2024*, March 31, 2024.

26. National Credit Union Administration, *1984 Annual Report*.

27. National Credit Union Administration, *Quarterly Credit Union Data Summary Q1 2024*.

28. National Credit Union Administration, *1984 Annual Report*.

29. Federal Financial Institutions Examination Council, Reports of Condition and Income Aggregated Data.

30. National Credit Union Administration, *Quarterly Credit Union Data Summary Q1 2024*.

31. Federal Financial Institutions Examination Council, Reports of Condition and Income Aggregated Data.

32. Casey Tolan, Audrey Ash, and Rene Marsh, "The Nation's Largest Credit Union Rejected More than Half Its Black Conventional Mortgage Applicants," *CNN Business*, December 14, 2023, https://www.cnn.com/2023/12/14/business/navy-federal-credit-union-black-applicants-invs/index.html.

33. Aaron Klein, "Credit Unions Are Making Money Off People Living Paycheck to Paycheck," *Politico*, October 5, 2023. https://www.politico.com/news/magazine/2023/10/05/credit-unions-overdraft-fees-00119904.

34. National Credit Union Administration, "Minority Depository Institutions," June 12, 2024. https://ncua.gov/support-services/credit-union-resources-expansion/resources/minority-depository-institution-preservation/mdi.

Chapter 2. The Blueprint: Filling in the Gap with Intention

1. Aditya Aladangady, Andrew C. Chang, and Jacob Krimmel, "Greater Wealth, Greater Uncertainty: Changes in Racial Inequality in the Survey of Consumer Finances," October 23, 2023. https://www.federalreserve.gov/econres/notes/feds-notes/greater-wealth-greater-uncertainty-changes-in-racial-inequality-in-the-survey-of-consumer-finances-20231018.html.

2. Board of Governors of the Federal Reserve System, "Bank Holding Companies and Financial Holding Companies," Partnership for Progress: A Program for Minority Depository Institutions from the Board of Governors of the Federal Reserve System, June 2007. https://www.fedpartnership.gov/bank-life-cycle/grow-shareholder-value/bank-holding-companies.

3. Broadway Financial Corporation, "2022 Benefit Report." Last accessed July 21, 2024. https://www.cityfirstbank.com/sites/default/files/2023-12/BenefitReport2023-2a%20FINAL%20.pdf.

4. Coalition to Save the South Shore Country Club Archives, [Box 15, Folder 13], Chicago Public Library, Woodson Regional Library, Vivian G. Harsh Research Collection of Afro-American History and Literature. Last accessed July 21, 2024. https://www.chipublib.org/fa-coalition-to-save-the-south-shore-country-club-csssc-archives/.

5. US Department of the Treasury, "CDCI Program Status." Last accessed July 21, 2024. https://home.treasury.gov/data/troubled-assets-relief-program/bank-investment-programs/cdci.

6. US Department of the Treasury Community Development Financial Institutions Fund, "CDFI Certification Application," December 2023. https://www.cdfifund.gov/sites/cdfi/files/2023-12/Final_508_CDFI_Certification_Application_Form_120523.pdf.

7. US Department of the Treasury Community Development Financial Institutions Fund, "List of Certified Community Development Financial Institution (CDFIs) with Contact Information as of June 17, 2024," June 17, 2024. https://www.cdfifund.gov/sites/cdfi/files/2024-06/CDFI_Cert_List_06-17-2024_Final.xlsx.

8. Clifford Rosenthal, "Democratizing Finance: Origins of the Community Development Financial Institutions Movement" (FriesenPress, 2018), 354.

9. US Congress, House, *Riegle Community Development and Regulatory Improvement Act of 1994*, HR 3474, 103rd Congress, introduced in House November 11, 1993. https://www.congress.gov/bill/103rd-congress/house-bill/3474/.

10. US Congress, House, *Riegle-Neal Interstate Banking and Branching Efficiency Act of 1994,* HR 3841, 103rd Congress, introduced in House February 10, 1994. https://www.congress.gov/bill/103rd-congress/house-bill/3841/.

11. US Department of the Treasury Community Development Financial Institutions Fund, *Searchable Awards Database.* https://www.cdfifund.gov/awards/state-awards/awardee-profile/001BE002046?orgID=1232.

12. US Department of the Treasury Community Development Financial Institutions Fund, *Searchable Awards Database.*

13. US Department of the Treasury Community Development Financial Institutions Fund, *Searchable Awards Database.* https://www.cdfifund.gov/awards/state-awards/awardee-profile/971BE000748?orgID=2134; https://www.cdfifund.gov/awards/state-awards/awardee-profile/981BE000096?orgID=2134; https://www.cdfifund.gov/awards/state-awards/awardee-profile/991BE001330?orgID=2134.

14. Office of the Comptroller of the Currency Community Affairs Department, "Bankers' Guide to the SBA 7(a) Loan Guaranty Program," *Community Development Insights,* December 2014. https://www.occ.gov/publications-and-resources/publications/community-affairs/community-developments-insights/pub-insights-dec-2014.pdf.

15. "2021 Report on Firms Owned by People of Color: Based on the 2020 Small Business Credit Survey," Small Business Credit Survey, Federal Reserve Banks, 2021. https://doi.org/10.55350/sbcs-20210415.

16. US Department of the Treasury Community Development Financial Institutions Fund, "CDFI Fund Releases Application Demand for FY 2024 Round of CDFI Program and NACA Program," March 15, 2024. https://www.cdfifund.gov/news/573.

Chapter 3. The Greenprint: Finding Community in Values

1. California Public Utilities Commission, "California Distributed Generation Statistics," April 30, 2024. https://www.californiadgstats.ca.gov.

2. Drew Desilver, "Most U.S. Bank Failures Have Come in a Few Big Waves," Pew Research Center, April 11, 2023.https://www.pewresearch.org/short-read/2023/04/11/most-u-s-bank-failures-have-come-in-a-few-big-waves/.

3. Federal Deposit Insurance Corporation, Historical Bank Data. https://banks.data.fdic.gov/bankfind-suite/historical.

4. Gary Groff, "Case Study: How to Grow Without Compromising Your Mission," *Triple Pundit*, July 14, 2014. https://www.triplepundit.com/story/2014 /case-study-how-grow-without-compromising-your-mission/42506.

5. Dan Fost, "*A Movement and a Market Converge at a Bank,*" *New York Times*, May 21, 2008. https://www.nytimes.com/2008/05/21/business/small business/21bank.html.

6. Amalgamated Financial Corporation, *2022 ESG Summary*, New York, NY, 2022. https://amalgamatedbank.com/sites/default/files/2022_CSR _Report.pdf.

7. Solar Energy Industries Association, *Solar Data Cheat Sheet*, Washington, DC, June 6, 2024. https://www.seia.org/cheatsheet.

8. California Public Utilities Commission, "California Distributed Generation Statistics," April 30, 2024. https://www.californiadgstats.ca.gov.

Chapter 4. New Community Banks and Credit Unions in Communities of Color

1. Deonna Anderson, "Creating a Black-Led Credit Union in Response to Police Violence," *NextCity*, May 18, 2018. https://nextcity.org/urbanist -news/creating-a-black-led-credit-union-in-response-to-police-violence.

2. National Credit Union Administration, *Annual Report 1986*, 1986.

3. National Credit Union Administration, *Annual Report 1986*.

4. Annual reports from the National Credit Union Administration, 2012–2022.

5. *Community Reinvestment Act of 1977*, Title VIII of Public Law 95–128; 91 Stat. 1147; 12 U.S.C. 2901 et seq. https://www.govinfo.gov/content/pkg /COMPS-258/pdf/COMPS-258.pdf.

6. Robert Kuttner, "The Reinvestment Movement vs. the Bankers," *American Prospect*, September 22, 2022. https://prospect.org/power/reinvestment -movement-vs-the-bankers/.

7. C. M. Tolbert et al., "Restructuring of the Financial Industry," *Rural Sociology* 79 (2014): 355–79. https://doi.org/10.1111/ruso.12037.

8. US Library of Congress, Congressional Research Service, *The Effectiveness of the Community Reinvestment Act*, Darryl E. Getter, author, 2020. https:// crsreports.congress.gov/product/pdf/R/R43661.

9. Anne Leland Clark, "Payday Loan Debts Have Financially Hobbled Thousands of Minnesotans," *Sahan Journal*, February 24, 2022. https:// sahanjournal.com/community-voices/payday-loan-predatory-debt -reform-minnesota-commentary/.

10. Center for Responsible Lending, *36% Cap on Annual Interest Rate Stops Payday Lending Debt Cycle*, November 2023. https://www.responsiblelend ing.org/research-publication/36-cap-annual-interest-rate-stops-payday -lending-debt-cycle.

11. Martha Stoddard, "Payday Lenders Disappeared from Nebraska after Interest Rate Capped at 36%," *Omaha World-Herald*, October 18, 2023.

12. Meredith Covington and Jennifer Johnson, "Into the Light: A Survey of Arkansas Borrowers Seven Years after State Supreme Court Bans Usurious Payday Lending Rates," *Policy Points*, vol. 43, Southern Bancorp Community Partners, April 2016. https://banksouthern.com/wp-content/uploads /2009/08/sbcp_policy-points-vol-43-payday-lending_20160516.pdf.

13. Minnesota Department of Commerce, *2021 Minnesota Payday Lending Data*, 2021. https://docs.google.com/spreadsheets/d/1YgR-Qty4uJuIJK CEzl4RcEgyd10leyDP3kPZ7H6wKYI/edit#gid=612432273.

14. Minnesota Department of Commerce, *2021 Minnesota Payday Lending Data*.

15. Grace Deng, "Payday Loans Trap Minnesotans in a Cycle of Debt," *Minnesota Reformer*, March 22, 2023.

16. Alex Horowitz and Chase Hatchett, "Credit Union Small-Dollar Loan Volume Hit New High in 2022," Pew Charitable Trusts, March 31, 2023. https://pew.org/3ZwUNl7.

17. US Small Business Administration, *7(a) and 504 Summary Report*, July 19, 2024. https://careports.sba.gov/views/7a504Summary/Report?:embed=yes &:toolbar=no.

18. US Small Business Administration. *Paycheck Protection Program Information Sheet for Lenders*. https://home.treasury.gov/system/files/136/PPP%20 Lender%20Information%20Fact%20Sheet.pdf.

19. US Department of Health, Education, and Welfare. Project Moneywise: Role of the Credit Unions in the War on Poverty, text, March 1967, accessed July 22, 2024 (https://texashistory.unt.edu/ark:/67531/metapth595318/); University of North Texas Libraries, The Portal to Texas History (https:// texashistory.unt.edu), crediting Texas Southern University.

20. Anne Hamilton, "Project Moneywise," *Social Security Bulletin* 32, no. 5 (May 1969), Social Security Administration.

21. National Credit Union Administration, *Annual Report 1986*, 1986.

22. Federal Deposit Insurance Corporation, *2021 FDIC National Survey of Unbanked and Underbanked Households*, 2021.

23. US Department of Commerce Bureau of the Census, Population Estimates Program (PEP), updated annually. Last accessed July 21, 2024. https://www.census.gov/quickfacts/fact/table/franklincountyohio/PST045222.

Chapter 5. New Banks and Credit Unions for the Environment

1. Inclusiv, "Community Development Credit Unions Will Deliver GGRF's Equity and Climate Goals," June 21, 2023. https://inclusiv.org/wp-con tent/uploads/2023/07/Inclusiv.GGRF-Handout-for-Senate-Climate -Change-Task-Force.June-21-2023.pdf.
2. Zoe Sullivan, "Puerto Rico Credit Unions Want a Solar-Powered Recovery," *Next City*, March 13, 2018.
3. Climate First Bank, "Climate First Bank Reduces Solar Loan Rates for Increased Access to Sustainable Living," GlobeNewswire News Room, February 26, 2024. https://www.globenewswire.com/en/news-release /2024/02/26/2835197/0/en/Climate-First-Bank-Reduces-Solar-Loan -Rates-for-Increased-Access-to-Sustainable-Living.html.
4. Yvon Chouinard, *Let My People Go Surfing: The Education of a Reluctant Businessman* (New York: Penguin, 2006).
5. US SIF "Trends Report" documents sustainable investment assets of $8.4 trillion, December 13, 2022. https://www.ussif.org/blog_home.asp ? Display=194.
6. Federal Deposit Insurance Corporation, *Banker Resource Center: Mutual Institutions*, 2023. https://www.fdic.gov/resources/bankers/mutual-institu tions/index.html.
7. Reports of Condition and Income, March 2024. Reported to the Federal Financial Institutions Examination Council on a quarterly basis.

Chapter 6. Tilting the Landscape Back Where We Need It

1. La-Brina Almeida, "A History of Racist Federal Housing Policies," Massachusetts Budget and Policy Center, August 6, 2021. https://massbudget.org/2021/08/06/a-history-of-racist-federal-housing-policies/.
2. Nicole Hannah-Jones, "Living Apart: How the Government Betrayed a Landmark Civil Rights Law," *ProPublica*, June 25, 2015.
3. Sarah Jane Gates, "More Lives than a Cat: A State and Federal History of Bank Deposit Insurance in the United States, 1829–1933," PhD diss., University of North Carolina at Greensboro, 2017.

4. Federal Deposit Insurance Corporation Division of Research and Statistics, "A Brief History of Deposit Insurance in the United States," prepared for the International Conference on Deposit Insurance, Washington, DC, September 1998.

5. Federal Deposit Insurance Corporation Division of Research and Statistics, "A Brief History."

6. Drew Desilver, "Most U.S. Bank Failures Have Come in a Few Big Waves," Pew Research Center, April 11, 2023. https://www.pewresearch.org/short-reads/2023/04/11/most-u-s-bank-failures-have-come-in-a-few-big-waves/.

7. Desilver, "Most U.S. Bank Failures."

8. Gates, "More Lives than a Cat."

9. Desilver, "Most U.S. Bank Failures."

10. Federal Deposit Insurance Corporation, "Bank Failures and Assistance Data." https://banks.data.fdic.gov/explore/failures.

11. Federal Deposit Insurance Corporation, "Bank Failures and Assistance Data."

12. Federal Deposit Insurance Corporation, "Bank Failures and Assistance Data."

13. US Library of Congress Congressional Research Service, *Silicon Valley Bank and Signature Bank Failures*, Andrew P. Scott and Marc Labonte, authors, March 21, 2023. https://crsreports.congress.gov/product/pdf/IN/IN12125.

14. Federal Financial Institutions Examination Council, Reports of Condition and Income Aggregated Data, December 31, 2022.

15. Federal Financial Institutions Examination Council, Reports of Condition and Income Aggregated Data, March 31, 2023.

16. Federal Financial Institutions Examination Council, Reports of Condition and Income Aggregated Data, March 31, 2024.

17. Federal Deposit Insurance Corporation, "Bank Application Actions." https://www.fdic.gov/regulations/applications/actions.html.

18. Xylex Mangulabnan and Nick Albicocco, "De Novo Bank Boom Hindered by Elevated Capital Requirements," S&P Global Market Intelligence, September 8, 2022. https://www.spglobal.com/marketintelligence/en/news-insights/latest-news-headlines/de-novo-bank-boom-hindered-by-elevated-capital-requirements-71828705.

19. Mangulabnan and Albicocco, "De Novo Bank Boom Hindered."
20. "Ponce Financial Group, Inc. Issues $225 Million of Preferred Stock to the U.S. Department of Treasury under the Emergency Capital Investment Program," June 9, 2022. https://poncebank.gcs-web.com/news-re leases/news-release-details/ponce-financial-group-inc-issues-225-million -preferred-stock-us.
21. US Department of the Treasury, "ECIP-Participants-September-2022. xlsx," *Emergency Capital Investment Program Archives*, 2023. https://home .treasury.gov/policy-issues/coronavirus/assistance-for-small-businesses /emergency-capital-investment-program/archives.
22. Matt Hanauer et al., "Community Banks' Ongoing Role in the U.S. Economy," *Federal Reserve Bank of Kansas City Economic Review*, June 24, 2021. https://doi.org/10.18651/er/v106n2hanauerlytlesummersziadeh.
23. Howard Bodenhorn and David Cuberes, "Finance and Urbanization in Early Nineteenth-Century New York," *Journal of Urban Economics* 104 (2018): 47–58. https://doi.org/10.1016/j.jue.2018.01.001.

Conclusion

1. National Credit Union Administration, "History of United States Currency: From the 1700s to Today," MyCreditUnion.gov, 2023.
2. Anjan V. Thakor and Edison G. Yu, "Funding Liquidity Creation by Banks," Olin Business School Center for Finance and Accounting Research Paper No. 2022/08, January 30, 2023. Available at SSRN: https:// ssrn.com/abstract=4104804 or http://dx.doi.org/10.2139/ssrn.4104804.
3. Federal Deposit Insurance Corporation, "Ratios for Community and Noncommunity Banks," *Quarterly Banking Profile*, March 31, 2024.
4. National Credit Union Administration, *1984 Annual Report*, 1984.
5. Federal Deposit Insurance Corporation, "BankFind Database," March 2024.
6. National Credit Union Administration, *Quarterly Credit Union Data Summary 2024 Q1*, March 21, 2024.
7. "Fossil Fuel Finance Report 2024," *Banking on Climate Chaos*, 2024. https://www.bankingonclimatechaos.org.

Acknowledgments

To my mom and dad, thank you for always letting your kids set their own course in life and holding them accountable to their own dreams. Thank you to my elementary school teachers; I can't believe how lucky I was to have you all: Ms. Fullard, Ms. Johnson, Ms. March, Ms. Hopkins/Marincola, Ms. Bullen, and my sixth-grade teacher Mr. Wilson, who first lit the writer's fire in me with those daily journal prompts like "Am I my brother's keeper?" Thank you to my mentors at Villanova University: Terry Nance, Walidah Justice, Maghan Keita, Carol Anthony, and Kathy Overturf, who never wavered in their belief in our ability to challenge power and infuse change into every community where we might end up.

My thanks also go to Aysha Khan, Deonna Anderson, Rachel Kaufman, Janine White, Kelsey Thomas, and Ariella Cohen, my editors over the years at Next City, the media outlet that made me into the journalist I am today. Thank you all for letting me follow my curiosity about how money, banking, and finance work to shape and reshape cities. Thank you for helping me grow as writer and for keeping me in check when I went a little too far into the weeds or tolerating it when I filed a few thousand more words than I was supposed to file. I thank Sara Schuenemann, Lucas Grindley, Melissa Simpson, Eleanor Barba, Eric

Shaw, and all of my current and former Next City colleagues. On top of having a stable place of employment as a journalist during this time of media industry upheaval, it's been such an honor and a pleasure having so many adventures with you. Thanks also go to Shawn Escoffery, and the Surdna Foundation, who made it possible for Next City to hire me back in 2015. And many thanks to Next City's readers for camaraderie, encouragement, feedback, and every form of support, including sharing our work out on those mean social media streets. I know it's not the healthiest thing, but journalists really do like to see it.

I thank Samira Rajan, Rachel Macarthy, Carlos Naudon, Barbara Arroyo, Arlo Washington, Charley Cummings, Vince Siciliano, Shannan Herbert, and so many others at all the community banks, credit unions and Community Development Financial Institutions whose work I've covered throughout the years. I thank Ron Grzywinski and Mary Houghton for their friendship, support, dinners, and lunches in Chicago and everything they taught me about community banks, their history, and the true public purpose they were always supposed to have. Juan Calixto, Angela Dowell, Lycrecia Parks, and the rest of the Chicago Community Loan Fund crew were always there to nerd out about community development finance with me; and Christina Jennings, Mark Fick, Brenda Pfahnl, and the Shared Capital Cooperative crew were always there to nerd out about cooperative economics and finance with me. My thanks go to Jessica Norwood, Nia Evans, Erika Seth Davies, Malia Lazu, Noni Session, Annie McShiras, Desi Danganan, Cathi Kim, Aaron Tanaka, Jessie Lee, Melonie Tharpe, Jaime Weisberg, Andrea Armeni, Eric Horvath, Kate Khatib, Alice Maggio, Anh-Thu Nguyen, Anton Seals, Deon Lucas, Cliff Rosenthal, and so many others I'm forgetting right now whose conversation and friendship continue to help me continually refine my understanding of race, money, power, and community.

Thanks to the Urban Design Forum and The Architectural League of New York, whose support under the New City Critics Fellowship was crucial to conceptualizing and workshopping ideas that eventually turned into this book.

I appreciate the help of Heather Boyer at Island Press, whose infinite patience and grace with me through this process has been a revelation.

And I thank Karalyn, Bennie, and Pepper for their love, for sharing their lives with me, and for helping me get through the hardest thing I've done so far.

Index

Pages indicating figures are in italics.

About the Author

Oscar Perry Abello is the senior economic justice correspondent at Next City, an independent not-for-profit digital media outlet covering solutions to advance social, racial, and environmental justice in cities across the United States. His writing has also appeared in *Yes!* magazine, *City & State New York*, *Impact Alpha*, *Shelterforce*, *Urban Omnibus*, and other outlets. Oscar is a child of immigrants descended from the former colonial subjects of the Spanish and US imperial regimes in the Philippines. He was born in New York City and raised in the inner-ring suburbs of Philadelphia. Oscar earned a bachelor's degree from Villanova University, where he majored in economics and minored in peace and justice studies. After several years embedded in the international development industry, he transitioned into journalism full-time in 2015. He currently lives in New York City with his domestic partner and the two most photogenic kitties in the world.